CISTERCIAN STUDIES SERIES: NUM

CW00555239

SAINT MARY OF EGYPT

Three Medieval Lives in Verse

CISTERCIAN STUDIES SERIES: NUMBER TWO HUNDRED-NINE

SAINT MARY OF EGYPT
Three Medieval Lives in Verse

Translated by
Ronald Pepin
and
Hugh Feiss OSB

Cistercian Publications
Kalamazoo, Michigan

The work of Cistercian Publications is made possible in part by support
from Western Michigan University to
The Institute of Cistercian Studies.

Library of Congress Cataloguing in Publication Data

Saint Mary of Egypt : three medieval lives in verse / translated by
Ronald Pepin and Hugh Feiss.
     p.   cm.
   ISBN-13: 978-0-87907-209-4
   ISBN-10: 0-87907-209-1
  1. Mary, of Egypt, Saint—Poetry—Translations into English.
2. Monasticism and religious orders—History—Middle Ages, 600–
1500. I. Pepin, Ronald E. II. Feiss, Hugh. III. Flodoard, of
Reims, 894–966. De triumphis Christi. English. Selections. IV.
Hildebert, Archbishop of Tours, 1056?–1133. Vita Beatae Mariae
Aegypticae. English. V. Vida de Santa María Egipcíaca. English.

PA8129.S25 2005
871'.03080351—dc22

                   2005033844

To Ellen, Joanne, Lynell, María, Rita, Sheila and Vanessa

Que vive en tal vida es de buena ventura (Berceo).

TABLE OF CONTENTS

FOREWORD

THE AIM OF THIS WORK is to make available in English three medieval metrical versions of the story of Saint Mary of Egypt. These three lives deal with some issues of perennial interest to monastics: communal and eremitical life; personal charism and institutional church; friendship between male and female monastics; and the complex of ideas connected with *penthos*-compunction-conversion. The lives have a wider interest as well for those interested in hagiography, in women's studies, in medieval literature, and in the heritage of Christianity.

This work has been a collaborative effort. The two latin lives were translated by Ron Pepin; the Spanish life was translated by Hugh Feiss. The introduction was written by Hugh Feiss, but it includes material and ideas supplied by Ron Pepin. The translations follow the structure of the originals, but they are not versified. They aim to be literal enough to convey the meaning and something of the literary style of the original authors.

This project has been made possible through the help of many people and libraries. Particularly deserving of mention are Professor Anna Minore, who took time to provide us with copies of hard-to-find material; Professor Carmen Wyatt-Hayes, who made available a copy of the chapter of her dissertation devoted to the Spanish life of Mary of Egypt translated here; Margot King, friend, scholar and publisher, who initially encouraged this project; Heather McKean, who painted the icon reproduced on the cover; E. Rozanne Elder whose kindness and editorial skills make Cistercian Publications a wonderful service to both the academy and the monastery; and Vanessa Butterfield, who proof read the introduction with great care. More than most projects, this one has made the translators aware of how much each scholarly endeavor is a collaboration not only with immediate associates but also with scholars and writers, known and unknown, separated from us by great distances of time and space. We thank them all.

We also thank Saint Mary of Egypt, who, though she may not agree with all that has been said about her here, surely must have been watching over us. Mary of Egypt's present intercession is verified by a story that Heather McKean told us. To a homeless man asleep in a dumpster a woman appeared in the night. She told him to go to a local parish, where he would be helped in finding food, clothing, shelter, and a job. The next day he went, and the parish did what the lady said they would. In the church there was an icon of Mary of Egypt. When the priest asked the man who had sent him to the church, he pointed to the icon and said: 'She is the one who came to the dumpster'.

THE STORY OF MARY OF EGYPT AND THE TEXTS

MARY OF EGYPT was a hermit. The story of her life was written to edify monks. After being penned around 600 AD, her story was translated, first into Latin by Paul the Deacon and others, and then into vernacular languages, of which the french and spanish versions are of particular interest here. Although these vernacular versions seem to be directed in part at monks, they also envisaged a larger audience. In this way, Mary of Egypt, who for most of her life was a pilgrim, traveled after her death from Palestine to Europe, from Greek to Latin to French to Spanish, and from the monastery to the secular world.

THE MONASTIC SETTING

Saint Benedict wrote his *Rule* in the second quarter of the sixth century. By then the heroic age of the earliest monks was several centuries in the past. Benedict looked back with admiration on those monastic heroes. He sketched out a modest rule for beginners. For those of his readers in a hurry to reach the fullness of monastic living there were the teachings and lives of the holy fathers (RB 73).[1] Those early founders taught that monks should not drink wine,[2] but monks of Benedict's time could not be persuaded of

---

[1] See the text and commentary in Terrence Kardong, *Benedict's Rule: A Translation and Commentary* (Collegeville: Liturgical Press, 1996) 602–619. It is not obvious what monastic fathers Benedict had in mind.

[2] For example, the elder mentioned by John Moschos, *The Spiritual Meadow*, 17, translated John Wortley, Cistercian Studies 193 (Kalamazoo: Cistercian Publications, 1992) 12.

that (RB 41.6). Monks of old said one hundred fifty psalms a day, but Benedict asked for no more than one hundred fifty a week (RB 18.25).

In the second half of the sixth century, two men were born who, like Benedict, were in search of monastic perfection, and who, like him, would influence the future of monasticism by their writings. One, John Moschos, traveled the Mediterranean world looking for exemplary monks.[3] He and his friend, Sophronius, who later became Patriarch of Jerusalem, wrote accounts of monastics who could serve as models for monks of their time. One such model was Mary of Egypt. To appreciate her, one needs to understand her setting and that of the author of her story, and this requires that one start at the beginning with the first monks. Three areas in the geography of early monasticism are particularly important for the story of Mary of Egypt: Egypt, Asia Minor, and Palestine. Three dimensions of monastic life in these geographic areas are particularly important for the story of her life: the variety of monastic lifestyles; the relation of men and women in early monasticism; and the place of monasticism in the institutional church.

Egypt

Saint Antony is said to have died in 356 at a very advanced age. When, as a young man, he decided to become a monk, he placed his sister in the charge of some respected virgins. Amoun, his disciple, was the first to settle at Nitria, forty miles southeast of Alexandria. Amoun arrived there about 315 AD, and then established Kellia about 338. It is reported that Amoun had been forced to marry when he was a young man, but he told his new wife that he would not consummate the marriage. His form of monastic life consisted of loosely connected groups of solitaries. Scetis, another fifty miles further south, was established by Macarius the Great

---

[3] *Spiritual Meadow*, xvii–xix.

(300–390 AD) around 335. Cassian, who brought the teachings of the eastern anchorites to the Latin-speaking West, lived at Scetis from about 385 to 399. These monastic settlements flourished until the end of the fourth century, when theological controversy and raiding desert nomads invaded their solitudes.

Meanwhile, after seven years' training under an ascetic named Palamon, Pachomius (290–346) founded, directed, and legislated for communal or cenobitic monasticism. The first of his well-organized institutions was located in a deserted village in upper Egypt. Near his monasteries for men he also established a monastery for women, where his sister Maria was the community's mother and elder, assisted by monks assigned to the task.

Although one reason monks had gone to the harsh and sparsely populated places of the egyptian desert was to escape the temptations of women, women came to visit them and even to live in the desert near them. Other dedicated women—virgins, widows, and penitents—resided in towns or villages where they lived in their family homes, independently, with a monk or cleric, or in communities; or they simply became wanderers on perpetual pilgrimage. Some of these women—for example Sarah, Theodora, and Syncletica—seem to have been teachers whose sayings are included among the collections of sayings of the desert monastics. Some instances are noted of highly advanced monastics who no longer noticed gender differences.[4] Devout women could become athletes of Christ, manly women.[5]

[4] See, for example, the story of the priest Conon in Moschos, *Spiritual Meadow*, 3; Wortley, 5–6.

[5] Susanna Elm, '*Virgins of God*': *The Making of Asceticism in Late Antiquity* (Oxford: Clarendon, 1994) 227–372; Joseph Patrich, *Sabas, Leader of Palestinian Monasticism: A Comparative Study in Eastern Monasticism, Fourth to Seventh Centuries* (Washington, DC: Dumbarton Oaks, 1995) 11–22. For other surveys of the rise of monasticism in the East, see also Derwas Chitty, *The Desert a City* (Oxford: Oxford University Press–Crestwood: St Vladimir's Seminary Press, 1996); *RB 80: The Rule of Benedict*, ed. Timothy Fry (Collegeville: Liturgical Press, 1981) 3–41.

Asia Minor

In Asia Minor monasticism developed rapidly during the fourth century, at a time when the Church was struggling with the doctrine of the Trinity. Here, too, many ascetics were city dwellers who lived in their family homes, with other ascetics, or even alone. Eustathius (300–377), who was later associated with condemned trinitarian views, was one of the pioneers of ascetical life in Asia Minor and Armenia. Basil, bishop of Ancyra (336–358), wrote a treatise on virginity in which he urged virgins to live well-disciplined lives and to contemplate only what pleased their Lord. Yet he taught that virgins are locked away, not to induce in them hatred of men, but that they might speak chastely with men associated with their way of life. Men and women ascetics should aim to become like angels; when they have eliminated sexual lust, they can cohabit through virtue.

In contrast to the rather anarchic enthusiasm of the early ascetical experiments in Asia Minor, the wide-ranging ecclesiastical program of Basil of Caesarea ('the Great', † 379) included an effort to legislate for a communal form of monasticism. Two of Basil's siblings, Macrina and Naucratius, had embraced the ascetical life on the family's rural estates near Annesi even before Basil did. Macrina gradually turned her household into a community of ascetics which included not only her former slaves, but poor girls left orphaned by famines. According to her brother, Gregory of Nyssa, she functioned as superior and teacher for her community. Naucratius, on the other hand, lived a more solitary ascetical life nearby. Basil's program for monastics was mildly ascetic and inserted them into the life of the local church, for which they provided hospitals and hostels. Basil aimed to define the subordinate role of ascetics in relation to the church hierarchy and to provide for separate institutions for male and female ascetics.[6]

---

[6] Elm, *Virgins*, 22–223; Patrich, *Sabas*, 11–22.

Palestinian Monasticism

The more immediate setting for the life of Mary of Egypt is Palestinian monasticism. The first monk in Palestine whose name is known was Hilarion, who was active at Thavatha near Gaza from 308. There a monastic community formed around him. Chariton, who came to Palestine as a pilgrim, brought monasticism to the Judean Desert when he founded his monastery at Pharan about 325. He later founded two lauras—monastic settlements in which the monks lived alone during the week, then gathered in church and dining hall on Saturday and Sunday. In the last third of the fourth century, a number of monasteries were built in Jerusalem. There was a monastery along the Kidron ravine, where Juvenal resided before becoming patriarch of Jerusalem in 425.

Euthymius († 473), arrived in Jerusalem from Melitene in Armenia in 405. Monastic life was already flourishing. He settled at Pharan for a time, then went to live in a cave with his friend Theoctistus. In 428 Euthymius founded a laura, and later several more monasteries. Two of his disciples, Martyrius and Elias, later became patriarchs of Jerusalem. Gerasimus founded a monastery along the Jordan around 455. Some hermits did the same at Calamon. In addition, there was a monastery at the church of Saint John the Baptist, which the Emperor Anastasius (491–518) erected at the site of Jesus' baptism. Its monks received an allowance from the imperial treasury. They cared for pilgrims and staffed the church.[7]

Originally, the monastic movement in Palesine was independent of the ecclesiastical hierarchy. When Patriarch Juvenal (422–458) appointed an auxiliary as archimandrite of the monks within his diocese, the monasteries were integrated into the ecclesiastical framework. The first to hold this office were monks from the monasteries of Jerusalem, but by 500 AD monks from the monasteries of the Judean

---

[7] John Binns, *Ascetics and Ambassadors of Christ: The Monasteries of Palestine*, 314–631 (Oxford: Clarendon, 1994); Yizhar Hirschfeld, *The Judean Desert Monasteries in the Byzantine Period* (New Haven: Yale, 1992).

Desert began to hold this office. Pre-eminent among them was Sabas.

According to the sympathetic life of Sabas by Cyril of Scythopolis (556), Sabas was born in Cappadocia in 439, and was raised in a monastery there. At eighteen he traveled to Palestine, where he spent twelve years in the monastery of Theoctistus. He then spent five years living in a cave, but returning to the monastery on weekends. During those years he accompanied his abbot, Longinus, when Longinus went to wish Euthymius well as the latter departed to spend Lent in the desert. Sabas sometimes joined them on their wanderings in the desert. After Euthymius' death in 473, Sabas became a wandering hermit in the desert, subsisting on wild plants. Those leading this type of wandering life were called 'grazers' (*boskoi*).[8] As we shall see, Mary of Egypt was one of them. Beginning in 483, Sabas founded the Great Laura. He worked in cooperation with several patriarchs of Jerusalem, but he several times met with strong opposition from his monks. He and his colleague Theodosius were appointed archimandrites in 492. Sabas died in 532.

Sabas was well acquainted with basilian monasticism and shared Basil's views about the integration of monasticism into the structures and life of the Church. Like Euthymius, however, Sabas was inclined to a more ascetical form of monasticism and admired the monks of Scetis. So, in his laura he combined elements of egyptian eremitical asceticism with the cenobitism of Saint Basil. Monasticism in the Judean Desert reached its zenith during the sixth century, and Sabas contributed much to its flowering.

> Before the lifetime of Sabas, the desert was unclaimed territory, a space at the end of the Empire where devils, beasts, and barbarians roamed. As a result of Sabas' shrewd opportunism and organizing

---

[8] Moschos, *Spiritual Meadow*, 19; Wortley, 13, with many further examples indicated on 238. Hirschfeld, *Judean Desert*, 214–215. Patrich, *Sabas*, 22, 42–43, 61, 293. Binns, *Ascetics*, 107–108.

abilities, the growing stream of pilgrims was diverted into this wasteland and settled in well-equipped and economically viable units. The new monastery-cities were part of the fabric of society, contributed to the economy, and helped secure the borders.[9]

The monasteries of Palestine were concentrated in and near Jerusalem. In the palestinian desert most monasteries were within two or three miles of another monastic settlement. They were connected with each other by trails, and most were within a day's travel from Jerusalem. The monasteries benefited from the prosperity and building activity under the emperor Justinian I (527–565). Many of them had houses in Jericho or Jerusalem, operated hospitals, and offered hospitality.[10]

The flowering of palestinian monasticism took place against a backdrop of ecclesiastical and political conflict. After the Council of Chalcedon in 451, there was a protracted struggle to win over 'monophysite' sympathizers to the christological teachings of the council. Another council held at Constantinople in 553 continued the negotiation of doctrinal agreement regarding Chalcedon and also condemned teachings of Origen and some of his followers. Politically, the eastern border of the Byzantine Empire was threatened by the Persians, who held Jerusalem from 614 to 631. In 638 the Arabs conquered and held the city.[11] Although the *Life of Mary of Egypt* seems to be set in the sixth century, these doctrinal and political struggles have few echoes in the *Life*. The monk Zosimas is said to have been orthodox in belief, and he tells Mary that all is well in church and state.

Monks in sixth- and seventh-century Palestine took inspiration from the writings, sayings, and lives of the monastic pioneers of the preceding two centuries, but also from

---

[9] Binns, *Ascetics*, 161–182 (quotation on 170); Hirschfeld, *Judean Desert*, 10.

[10] Binns, *Ascetics*, 80–94.

[11] Binns, *Ascetics*, 1–17, 183–217. The Origenists' power peaked in the decade after the deaths of Sabas (532) and Theodosius (529).

the lives of recent predecessors who provided models for encouragement and emulation and served to enhance the prestige of monasticism or of a specific monastery.[12] Many of the monastic models—Antony, Pachomius, Euthymius, Sabas—were persons who had embraced the monastic life at a young age, found excellent tutors, and advanced from strength to strength. There were, however, also converts who came to monastic life after years of dissipation. Some of these were reformed prostitutes, and among them Mary of Egypt was pre-eminent.

THE BEGINNINGS OF MARY'S STORY

The earliest mention of the story of Saint Mary of Egypt may occur in the *Life of Kyriakos* written by Cyril of Scythopolis near the middle of the sixth century.[13] Cyril, who also wrote the lives of Sabas and Euthymius, says that he heard the story of a hermit named Mary from a monk named John, who had encountered her living in a cave in the Judean Desert. She told John that she had been a singer at the Church of the Resurrection in Jerusalem before she departed for the desert to avoid being an occasion of sexual temptation for men. She had lived eighteen years in the desert on a jar of water and a basket of loaves. By the time John went back to visit Mary a second time, she was dead. He buried her in her hermit's cave. She had died not long before Cyril wrote about her.

[12] For the extant lives of the palestinian monks, see Binns, *Ascetics*, 23–55.

[13] Cyril of Scythopolis, *Lives of the Monks of Palestine*, translated R. M. Price, annotated by John Binns, Cistercian Studies 114 (Kalamazoo: Cistercian, 1991) 256–258. The relevant text is cited in Benedicta Ward, *Harlots of the Desert: A Study of Repentance in Early Monastic Sources*, Cistercian Studies 106 (Kalamazoo: Cistercian, 1987) 28–29. See also, Patrich, *Sabas*, 293; Hirschfeld, *Judean Desert*, 232–234. For bibliography on Mary of Egypt, see the works cited in these notes and *Bibliotheca sanctorum* (Rome: Città Nuova, 1967) 8:989–994.

For Cyril's sources, works, and style, see Binns, *Ascetics*, 56–76. Cyril was born at Scythopolis about 525. His family knew Saint Sabas. As a boy, Cyril was educated in the Bible and the lives of the saints. When he was about eighteen,

The next possible antecedent for Mary's story appears in *The Spiritual Meadow* of John Moschos (*c.* 540/550–*c.* 620).[14] He tells the story of an unnamed nun from Jerusalem. She went to the desert to avoid being the occasion of sexual temptations to some man. There she lived for seventeen years on a basket of vegetables. Many of the incidents in Sophronius' *Life of Mary of Egypt* are found elsewhere in Moschos' work, which is well stocked with friendly lions.[15]

SOPHRONIUS, LIFE OF MARY OF EGYPT

The classic version of Mary's story from which those translated here all descend is attributed to Sophronius (*c.* 560–638), who was patriarch of Jerusalem for the last five years

---

he became successively a lector and a monk. He went to Palestine, where he spent some months as a solitary in the desert at Calamon, before spending eleven years in the monastery of Euthymius. From 555 to 557 he was one of a group of orthodox monks who wrested control of the New Laura from the Origenists. In 557 he moved to the Great Laura which had been founded by Sabas, and died there sometime after 560. He was a strong supporter of Chalcedon and an opponent of the Origenists. He wrote seven lives of outstanding monks of the palestinian desert, including Chariton, Euthymius, and Sabas. His hagiographical work details the development of monastic life in Palestine from 400 to 550.

Kyriakos (Cyriac), a younger contemporary of Sabas, was born in Corinth and died at a very old age in 557. He spent time in the laura of Euthymius and the monastery of Gerasimus. Beginning in 526, he lived for several long periods as a hermit in the desert.

[14] Moschos, *Spiritual Meadow*; Wortley, 148–149. See Binns, *Ascetics*, 49–53. Moschos takes up the story of the Palestinian monks where Cyril of Scythopolis left off, around 550. John Moschos was a great traveler. He began his monastic career at the monastic community of Theodosius, then went to the laura of Pharan. He visited Egypt, then returned to live in several palestinian lauras. When the Persian threat increased in Palestine, he traveled to Antioch, Egypt, Cyprus and Samos, and finally to Rome, where he died. His body was brought back to Palestine by his friend Sophronius, who later became Patriarch of Jerusalem.

[15] Jane Stevenson, 'The Holy Sinner: The Life of Mary of Egypt', *The Legend of Mary of Egypt in Medieval Insular Hagiography*, edd. Erich Poppe and Bianca Ross (Dublin: Four Courts Press, 1996) 30–33.

of his life.[16] In the eighth century this life was cited by Saint John of Damascus in one of his discourses in defense of images. Sophronius' *Life of Mary of Egypt* has never been critically edited, in part because of the great number of extant manuscripts. When he expanded Mary's story and made her an egyptian harlot, Sophronius may have been influenced by Ezekiel 23:2-3, which speaks of a mother and daughter who were whores in Egypt and stood for unfaithful Samaria and Jerusalem. Another influence was Jerome's *Life of Paul, the First Hermit*, in which Antony goes in search of a teacher more perfect than himself—as Zosimas does in *The Life of Mary of Egypt*. Jerome's tale also ends with the story of grave-digging lions.[17]

Sophronius' account of Mary's life had great success. It was incorporated into the greek liturgy for Lent.[18] The

[16] *Acta Sanctorum*, April 1, Appendix, pp. xi–xviii. J. P. Migne, *Patrologia cursus completus. Series graeca*, 87/3:3697–3725. Hereafter Migne's *Patrologia* will be cited as PG and PL. Sophronius was born about 560. After completing his education, he visited the monks in Egypt, then lived as a monk in Palestine. He became Patriarch of Jerusalem in 634 and died in 639. For these dates, see Christoph von Schönborn, *Sophrone de Jérusalem: Vie monastique et confession dogmatique*, Théologie historique 10 (Paris: Beauchesne, 1972) 97. Sophronius wrote dogmatic works, sermons, liturgical and other poetry, and hagiographical works about the Alexandrians Cyrus and John, and John the Almoner. Schönborn, p. 116, gives several reasons why the *Life of Mary of Egypt* should not be attributed to Sophronius: 1) ancient sources cite the work as anonymous; 2) the style is not that of Sophronius; 3) one source of *The Life of Mary of Egypt* is John Moschos' *Spiritual Meadow*. As we have seen, the story there is different from that in the *Life*. It seems unlikely that Sophronius would have contradicted his friend's account.

[17] Stevenson, 'Holy Sinner', 24, 27–28. Manuel Alvar, *Vida de Santa María Egipciaca* (Madrid: Consejo Superior de Investigaciones Científicas, 1970–1972) 1:13–14, summarizes a number of points of correspondence between the two works. These were noted in the pioneering studies of F. Delmas.

[18] Saint Andrew of Crete, *The Great Canon: The Life of St. Mary of Egypt*, ed. and translated by Sister Katherine and Sister Thekla (Normanby, Whitby, North Yorkshire: Greek Orthodox Monastery of the Assumption, 1974) 66–84. 'Canon of Mary of Egypt' in *The Lenten Triodion*, translated Mother Mary and Bishop Kallistos Ware (London, 1979) 447–463. E. Makris Walsh, 'The Ascetic Mother Mary of Egypt', *Greek Orthodox Theological Review* 34 (1989) 56–69. I owe the last two references to Jane Stevenson, 'The Holy Sinner: The Life of

Second Council of Nicaea (787) attributed the work to Sophronius and commented that it is 'full of compunction and offers much consolation to the lapsed and sinners, if they wish to desist from their evil deeds'.[19] The text was deeply rooted in its setting. As we noted, the monastery of John the Baptist on the Jordan River actually existed.[20] There really was an icon of Mary at the church of the Holy Sepulcher. The theme of the converted prostitute occurs in the lives of Pelagia and Thaïs, both of which were composed about the same time.[21]

Mary of Egypt', 19. According to Ward, *Harlots*, 26, in the eastern liturgy for the fifth Sunday of Lent, Saint Mary of Egypt is presented as a model of repentance, and her life is read at Matins on Thursday of that week. A photocopied order of service for Saint John of Damascus Russian Orthodox Chruch in Poway, California, for Sunday, 21 April 2002, contains three stanzas addressed to Mary of Egypt. They tell about her conversion in Jerusalem and then her life in the desert, where she 'erased the images of sin' from her soul. Now she stands before Christ in heaven and is asked to entreat him with boldness for those who pray to her. In explanatory notes in the back, Fr Matthias F. Wahba observes: 'Today, the Fifth Sunday in Lent, is for the Orthodox Church the Sunday of St. Mary of Egypt. . . . Here we have a story in which the sinner knows the heart of the saintly monk: in which a humble woman gives blessing to the worthy priest because he has seen that her own gifts of the Spirit exceed the ranks of ecclesiastical office; in which sanctity is found outside the monastery more than within; in which the desert, the place of death, becomes the place of life; in which the peace of God's kingdom is restored as the lion and the man become partners in piety.' *Prayers for Purity* (Astoria, New York: Greek Orthodox Church the Holy Protection of the Mother of God, n.d.) 32, includes a prayer to Mary of Egypt as a saint who by the cross overcame carnal temptation.

[19] PG 129:314–315, cited by Stevenson, 'Holy Sinner', 23–24; see also the references she gives, 20, note 11.

[20] There are four monasteries associated with churches along the pilgrimage road from Jerusalem to the site of Jesus' baptism. The monastery of Saint John the Baptist remained in continuous use until the Middle Ages. See Hirschfeld, *Judean Desert*, 16, 56–58, 62, 70, 254, 259. According to a description by Antoninus of Placentia (c. 570), the monastery was very large and maintained several hostels.

[21] Stevenson, 'Holy Sinner', 24–25. For a discussion and translation of these lives, see Ward, *Harlots*, 57–75 (Pelagia); 76–84 (Thaïs); for the theme of holy (converted) sinners, see Erhard Dorn, *Der Sündige Heilige in der Legende des Mittelalters* (Munich: Wilhelm Fink, 1967) especially 52–71. Elm, *Virgins*, 259–261, discusses the story of Paesia, another converted prostitute.

Benedicta Ward captures something of the drama and the theological significance of Sophronius' tale, which helped to make it extremely popular ever afterwards. An example of the dramatic flavor is the first meeting between Zosimas and Mary:

> Mary, alive and awake to life, is courteous when she meets the good, controlled, pious monk from a conventional monastic setting; she talks with him by moonlight, telling her story for the first time, always careful not to shock him; and Zossimas dazed with love and adoration, returns at her bidding, as docile and humble as a lover.
>
> But the story of Mary of Egypt is of deeper significance than simply a dramatic tale of lust turned into love. It is clearly packed with intricate symbols, the most important of which is the contrast of the good, self-satisfied monk who relies for salvation on his own works, with Mary the sinful woman who receives the simple gift of salvation from Christ without any acts, self-exploration, sacraments or prayers, but only because of her great need. Other symbols underline this central theme: Mary takes with her into the desert three loaves of bread which, like the loaves of the prophet Elijah, do not diminish; she passes over the water of the Jordan, the symbol of baptism; she is seen walking on the waters, and at peace with all creation; and it is a lion that comes out of the desert for her burial, the sign of the prince of peace.[22]

There will be opportunity to return to Sophronius' work in the discussion of the three poems that are presented below. In her recent scholarly translation, Mary Kouli divides the twenty-three pages of text into forty-one paragraphs.[23]

---

[22] Ward, *Harlots*, 33.

[23] *Holy Women of Byzantium: Ten Saints' Lives in English Translation*, Alice-Mary Talbot, ed. (Washington, DC: Dumbarton Oaks, 1996) 70–93.

What follows is an outline of Sophronius' *Life of Mary of Egypt*, keyed to those paragraphs, which will then serve as reference points for comparing later versions of the story with Sophronius' account.[24]

1. The author would be negligent if he did not recount what he knows of Mary. One should believe this story that he heard from a holy and truthful man.

2. There was a man named Zosimas who had lived in palestinian monasteries since his childhood. Zosimas was orthodox in belief and strict in monastic discipline. He taught others, studied the Bible, and said psalms. Some say he received a divine vision.

3. Zosimas said that when he was fifty-three years old, he became tempted to pride, thinking no one could still teach him anything about asceticism or contemplation. He was told to go to a monastery located near the river Jordan.[25]

4. The superior of that monastery received him. When Zosimas said he had come because he had heard that the abbot could bring one close to Christ, the abbot replied that only God can do that. Zosimas accepted the abbot's invitation to stay.

5. The monks there were very austere. They meditated on the Scriptures. Zosimas was edified by their efforts to recreate the divine paradise.

6. After many days, Lent arrived. At that isolated and strictly cloistered monastery it was the custom that at the

---

[24] For another summary retelling of Sophronius' *Life of Mary of Egypt*, see Virginia Burrus, *The Sex Lives of the Saints: An Erotics of Ancient Hagiography* (Philadelphia: University of Pennsylvania Press, 2004) 147–154.

[25] Palladius, *The Lausiac History*, 20, translated Robert T. Meyer, Ancient Christian Writers 34 (Westminster, Maryland: Newman, 1965) 70–71, tells of a monk who prayed continuously, but was discouraged to meet a virgin in a nearby village who surpassed him in her prayer and asceticism. The moral of that story is that purity of heart is what counts, not numbers. Burrus, *Sex Lives*, 148, comments that Zosimas went in search of a saintly father, but what he found was 'a "mother" who will not so much fulfil as intensify his longing and thereby finally—blissfully—shatter his self-satisfaction'.

beginning of Lent the monks participated in the Eucharist, ate a small amount of food, prayed in the chapel, kissed each other and embraced the abbot and received his blessing.

7. Then they all went out into the desert where they spent Lent in complete solitude. One or two monks stayed behind to minister in the church.[26] Each monk took a little food with him if he wished. They crossed the Jordan, and then each separated from the others, so each could live for himself and for God.

8. They returned on the Sunday before Easter. In order to avoid trying to impress others, they did not talk with each other about their time in the desert.

9. Zosimas, then, crossed the Jordan. He kept moving, stopping for the night wherever he happened to be. He hoped to find a holy hermit in the innermost desert. On the twentieth day he stopped to chant psalms.

10. He saw a shadowy figure appear on his right. He saw that it was a naked person, whose skin was blackened by the sun and whose hair was short and white. He ran after the figure, hoping to witness a great marvel.[27]

11. The other person fled, but Zosimas caught up enough to ask her to stop.[28]

12. The figure crossed a dry stream bed and went up the other side. Zosimas stood weeping on the opposite bank. The other addressed him by name, which she could only have known miraculously, saying she was ashamed to be naked. She asked for one of his cloaks.

---

[26] For the custom of monks going out from their monasteries to spend Lent in the desert, see Patrich, *Sabas*, 42–43, 47, 272, 293. Evidently, Euthymius began the custom of going to the desert during Lent. Binns, *Ascetics*, 105, notes that Lent coincided with the wettest part of the season, when vegetation was most abundant and the desert was therefore most hospitable to human visitors.

[27] Burrus, *Sex Lives*, 148–149, notes that Jerome (*Ep* 22.7) described skin dried out by the desert sun in terms reminiscent of Sg 1.6, and also that the white hair recalls Rv 1.13-14.

[28] Burrus, *Sex Lives*, identifies a similar chase scene in Jerome's *Life of Paul* 9.

13. With eyes averted, he threw it to her. They knelt, asking each other for a blessing. She said that Zosimas, a priest, should bless her first. Zosimas said she had obviously received great blessings and so should bless him.

14. She finally blessed him. She asked why he came, then quizzed him about conditions in church and state. He said all was well. He begged her prayers. She said she would obey his request.

15. She turned to the East to pray. She was elevated a cubit above the earth. Zosimas was terrified. She assured him she was flesh and blood and a baptized Christian; she made the sign of the cross.

16. Zosimas threw himself down, grasped her feet, and, weeping, asked her to tell him her whole life story.[29] He said, 'God seems to have brought me here so I can tell others about you'.

17. She raised him up and said: 'I am ashamed to tell you my sinful actions, but since you have seen my bare body, I shall lay bare to you also my deeds'. First, she made him promise to pray for her.

18. Mary came from Egypt. When she was twelve years old, she had abandoned her parents and gone to Alexandria, where she threw herself 'entirely and insatiably into the lust of sexual intercourse'. For more than seventeen years she was 'a public temptation to licentiousness'. She did not live wantonly just for money.[30] She supported herself by begging and spinning flax.

19. One day she saw a huge crowd of men running toward the sea to go to Jerusalem for the feast of the Exaltation of the Cross. She asked to go with them and offered her body

---

[29] Here there is clearly an echo, in reverse, of the gospel story of the sinful woman who bathed Jesus' feet with her tears (Lk 7.38). The gift of tears was highly esteemed in byzantine monasticism. See Stevenson, 'Holy Sinner', 36–38.

[30] Ward, *Harlots*, 27, cites William of Malmesbury, who catches the import of this: 'She was wicked simply for the fun of it.'

as payment. She wanted to go because she wanted a ready crowd of lovers.[31]

20. She approached some young men, offered herself, and made them laugh. She threw away her distaff, which she happened to be holding.

21. On the boat she lured the men into wanton acts. Once they landed, she did the same with the people in Jerusalem.

22. When the feast of the Exaltation of the Holy Cross came, she went with others to the church. She tried to go in, but some divine force held her back.[32]

23. After four attempts she was worn out and went and stood at the corner of the courtyard of the church. She realized that it was her sinfulness that kept her out.[33] She began to cry. She saw the icon of the Mother of God above where she was standing. She prayed to Mary, ever virgin, for help so she could enter the church and venerate the holy cross. She promised that once she saw the cross, she would

[31] Regarding pilgrimage among the early monks. see Elm, *Virgins*, 272–274, who notes that Alexandria was an important port of entry for pilgrims to the Holy Land. There was a road which spanned the two hundred miles between Alexandria and Jerusalem.

[32] Besides the obvious reference to the Garden of Eden, there are parallels in the lives of various saints. See Alvar, *Vida*, 1:15.

[33] Moschos, *Spiritual Meadow*, 48; Wortley, 39, tells of Cosmiana, who was unable to enter the Church of Christ's Resurrection because she was a Monophysite. The Virgin Mary told her that she could not enter until she was in communion with holy Church. Chapter 49 of the *Spiritual Meadow* tells a similar story about a man named Gebemer.

The dynamics of Mary of Egypt's conversion are not elaborated in Sophronius' account. Reflecting on Paul the Deacon's latin translation of Sophronius, Carmel M. Posa , 'Mary and Zossima: Icons of Mutuality in the Spiritual Journey', *Tjurunga* 57 (1999) 14–15, writes: 'Never rejected even by the unwilling, Mary's hunger eats its way towards Jerusalem. At the doors of the cathedral on the festival of the Exaltation of the Holy Cross she is faced with the mysterious and persistent inability to enter and see this holy relic of love. Physically thwarted, Mary experiences a deep sense of rejection for the first time in her life. She finally takes stock of her situation with her typical intensity and arrives at the cause of this rejection. . . . Unable to deal with this experience from out of her own resources, she throws herself at the feet of a nearby icon of the Mother of God and pleads for help.'

renounce the world and do whatever Mary, the guarantor of her salvation, might bid her to do.

24. Immediately she received the fire of faith. Encouraged by the compassionate Mother of God, she entered the church, saw the cross, and knew that God is always ready to accept repentance. She rushed back to the icon.

25. She thanked Mary for being her guarantor. She heard a voice saying that if she crossed the Jordan she would find a place of repose. She hurried away.

26. Someone gave her three coins, with which she bought three loaves of bread.[34] She reached the church of John the Baptist near the Jordan. She prayed in church and washed her face and hands in the holy water of the river.[35] She received the sacraments at the church, ate half a loaf, drank from the Jordan, and slept on the ground. Next day she crossed the river in a small boat. She let the Virgin Mary lead her into the desert.

27. That was forty-seven years ago. She lived off the three loaves of bread.

28. For the first seventeen years she battled irrational desires for food and wine. Lewd songs came into her mind. To combat these thoughts, she imagined herself in front of the icon of the Mother of God and prayed for her help.[36]

29. She struggled against sexual desires, and begged Mary for help 'for one who was in danger <of drowning> in the sea of the desert'.

---

[34] The three loaves have both trinitarian and eucharistic symbolism. Biblical allusions include Elijah, who lived forty days and forty nights on a hearth cake (1 Kgs 19.8), Saul (1 Sm 10.3), and the New Testament miracles of the multiplication of loaves (Mk 6.34-44; 8.1-10 par.). The spanish poet will follow Sophronius in saying that the loaves dried out, but he adds that later they turned white, a prodigy not mentioned in his french source (Alvar, *Vida*, 1:32).

[35] Posa, 'Mary and Zossima', 15, sees baptismal symbolism in this washing and refers to the story of Thekla baptizing herself.

[36] Mary lived her dissolute life for seventeen years. She spent the first seventeen years of her repentance battling temptations arising from memories and habits of those years.

30. After her loaves were gone, she lived off wild plants. Her clothes wore out, and she endured cold and heat. She fed and clothed herself with the word of God.

31. In the desert she never saw man or beast. She never learned to read, but the Word of God taught her. Having finished her story, she again asked Zosimas to pray for her. He fell weeping at her feet.

32. She made him promise not to tell anyone what she had told him until after her death. She asked him to leave her, but to come back the following year.[37] She asked him to tell Abbot John at the appropriate time that he should correct some matters in the monastery. Zosimas was to stay in the monastery until Holy Thursday, then bring the Body and Blood of Christ to her at the bank of the Jordan.

33. He waited impatiently in the monastery for a year. He was sick when Lent started so he had to stay inside.

34. On Holy Thursday he brought the Body and Blood of Christ in a small chalice, as well as a small amount of food. He waited on the bank of the Jordan, longing to see her, afraid that maybe his unworthiness prevented her from coming.

35. She appeared on the opposite bank, made the sign of the cross, and walked across the river. She would not let him bow before her. She asked him to recite the creed and the Our Father. She gave him the customary kiss of love on his mouth, received the sacraments, and prayed to the Lord that now she might depart in peace.

36. She asked Zosimas to return the next year to the dry stream bed where they had first met. He said he wished he could follow her from then on. She ate three lentils from the food he had brought. They asked each other for prayers. She walked across the river; he returned to the monastery, blaming himself for not asking her name.

---

[37] Mary's reluctance to have Zosimas stay longer may indicate that by the time her life was written there was a policy in Palestine to segregate monastics by gender.

37. A year later he returned to the desert. When he could not find her, he prayed that God would show him this 'inviolate treasure'. Then he spotted the blessed woman lying dead on the eastern slope, her hands folded properly, facing east.[38] He bathed her feet with his tears, for he did not dare touch any other part of her.

38. He prayed the appropriate psalms and prayers and wondered if he should bury her. Some writing on the ground by her head[39] stated that she had died on the same day that he had brought her communion and that he should bury her body there.

39. He wondered how he could bury her. A lion came, licked her feet, and indicated its benign intent. The lion dug a pit for the burial.[40]

40. With the lion in attendance, he covered her body with earth. Zosimas went back to his monastery and told everything that had happened. The monks celebrated the woman's memorial service with awe and affection. Abbot John corrected some monks who needed it.

41. The monks passed on the story of these events from one generation to the next, presenting her as a model. Now the author has put them into writing, evidently for the first time. The work closes with a doxology.

Duncan Robertson ranks the story of Mary of Egypt

> among the master-texts of hagiographical literature, along with the lives of Anthony and Paul of Thebes. Her legend dramatizes the most fundamental Christian themes: the value of contrition; the availability

---

[38] Palladius, *The Lausiac History*, 60; Meyer, 141, tells of a virgin who, having lived for sixty years as an ascetic with her mother, had a premonition of her own death. She died during the night and was found the next morning laid out for burial.

[39] For parallels, see Alvar, *Vida*, 1:16. Burrus, *Sex Lives*, 154, notes that Mary was illiterate and that the words had stayed visible in the sand for a whole year.

[40] For stories of Palestinian monks taming lions, see the references in Binns, *Ascetics*, 223, 229–231. Paul the Deacon added a preface which included a reference to Tobit, who was noteworthy for his charitable efforts to bury the dead.

of salvation to even the most egregious sinner; the power of an acknowledged dependence upon God's mercy, which qualifies her as a mystical teacher for Zosimas. She stands moreover, most mysteriously, as a figure for contemplation, associated (confusedly or deliberately) with her biblical namesakes, Mary Magdalene and Mary of Bethany. Her gratuitous sexuality, however explicitly condemned, mirrors the absolutely unmixed, spontaneous and irresistible desire for God which monastic exegesis ascribes to the bride of the Song of Songs.[41]

Paul the Deacon of Naples

In the West, Sophronius' *Life of Mary of Egypt* was translated into Latin early in the ninth century by Paul the Deacon of Naples. Paul's translation is elegant and faithful. He leaves out only the final authorial statement about the oral transmission of the story among the monks of Abbot John's monastery.[42]

In addition to Paul the Deacon's translation, there is an anonymous latin translation that has survived in at least two manuscripts. One of these is an eleventh-century collection of the *Lives of the Holy Fathers*.[43] The second manuscript was written in the last half of the tenth century in

---

[41] Duncan Robertson, *The Medieval Saints' Lives: Spiritual Renewal and Old French Literature*, Edward C. Armstrong Monographs on Medieval Literture, 8 (Lexington, Kentucky: French Forum Publishers, 1995) 104.

[42] Stevenson, 'Holy Sinner', 40–42. Stevenson edits Paul's life from three insular manuscripts (51–79) and provides a translation (80–98). Hugh Magennis, who judges Stevenson's edition and translation 'not reliable', gives his own in his *The Old English Life of Saint Mary of Egypt. An Edition of the Old English text with modern English parallel-text translation* (Exeter: University of Exeter Press, 2002). The edition in PL 73/1:671–690 is translated by Ward, *Harlots*, 35–56, and her translation is reprinted in *Medieval Saints: A Reader*, ed. Mary-Ann Stouck (Peterborough, Ontario: Broadview, 1999) 97–114.

[43] It was published in *Bibliotheca Casinensis*, vol. 3 (1877): *Florilegium Casinense*, 226–235.

Spain.[44] This Latin translation of Mary's life is less faithful
to Sophronius' version than Paul the Deacon's. Prose versions in Latin appeared in Vincent of Beauvais' *Speculum
historiale* and in the *Golden Legend*. Mary of Egypt's story
was related to the developing cult of the Blessed Virgin
Mary in Honorius Augustodunensis' sermon 'On the An-
nunciation' and in collections of miracles of the Virgin. In
these later accounts, which emphasize the power and mercy
of the Blessed Virgin Mary, the role of Zosimas shrinks.[45]
The story of Mary of Egypt was destined to be retold many
times in many languages, beginning with the *Old English
Life of Saint Mary of Egypt*.[46] At each stage, readers found
new meanings. Here, however, our concern is three metrical
versions of Mary's story. The three metrical versions translated in this volume illustrate the continuity and innovation
found in these later retellings; each has its own history and
each deserves its own introduction.

FLODOARD OF REIMS, 'ON MARY THE EGYPTIAN AND ZOSIMAS'

Flodoard, a canon of Reims, died in 966. His major work is a
history of the church at Reims *(Historia Remensis Ecclesiae)*;
he also composed in verse the three books of *De triumphis
Christi sanctorumque Palaestinae (On the Triumphs of Christ
and the Saints of Palestine)*, and other brief poetical works.

---

[44] See the discussion in Jerry R. Craddock, 'Apuntes para el estudio de la
Leyenda de Santa María Egipciaca en España' in *Homenaje a Rodriguez-Moriño*
(Madrid, 1966) 1:99–110.

[45] On other Latin versions see Peter F. Dembowski, ed., *La Vie de Sainte
Marie l'Égyptienne: versions en ancien et en moyen français* (Genève: Droz,
1977) 15–16; Robertson, 105; Magennis, 10–12.

[46] Magennis, *The Old English Life of Saint Mary of Egypt* (above, n. 42);
Leslie A. Donavan, *Women Saints' Live in Old English Prose*, The Library of
Medieval Women (Cambridge: D. S. Brewer, 1999) 97–120; Onnaca Heron,
'The Lioness in the Text: Mary of Egypt as Immasculated Female Saint', *Quid-
ditas* 21 (2000) 23–44.

His poem 'On Mary the Egyptian and Zosimas' occurs in Book One, chapter four, of *On the Triumphs of Christ and the Saints of Palestine.*[47]

Flodoard's poem is a condensed version of the life of Mary which Paul the Deacon translated from Sophronius. Flodoard quickly moves Zosimas out into the desert. When Zosimas catches up with Mary, he pleads with her to turn to him in the name of 'him who never rejected anyone'. This reference to divine mercy sounds the theme of the story, puts Zosimas in the position of one seeking mercy, and leads to the disclosure of Mary's nakedness. Zosimas refers to Mary as 'mother', a term which recalls the title *'amma'* used for holy women of the early monastic movement. She makes the sign of the cross on her forehead, lips, and breast. He urges her to tell him her story, because God must have brought him to her for that reason.

Mary recounts her misdeeds briefly, emphasizing that it was for her own pleasure that she took the initiative in leading men astray. When she went to join the pilgrims, she threw away her distaff and spindle (Sophronius and Paul the Deacon mention only one of these instruments). By leaving them behind, she deprived herself of what had been an upright and womanly source of income. She will rely solely on her harlotry for a while. In Jerusalem on the feast of the Exaltation of the Holy Cross, she cannot enter the church. She begs Mary, mistress of heaven, to let her see the sacred cross on which her Son died for sinners. In return, she promises amendment. From that moment her conversion rapidly deepens. She then speaks of her subsequent seventeen years of struggle against temptation in the desert. She seems to have conquered her yearnings by turning to Blessed Mary who reminded her of divine judgment, but also guided her

[47] Flodoard's *Historia* was edited, with an introduction, bibliography and 'une relecture de Flodoard', by F. Châtillon in *Revue du Moyen Age latin* 37 (1981) v–xxxiv and 1–220. The metrical works are printed in PL 135. Peter Jacobsen, *Flodoard von Reims: Sein Leben und seine Dichtung, 'De triumphis Christi'* (Leiden, 1978) was not available to us.

and brought her solace. According to Sophronius (and Paul the Deacon), after receiving communion Mary traveled in one hour to a place which it took Zosimas twenty days to reach; Flodoard changes these figures to three hours and ten days. Like Paul the Deacon, Flodoard does not include Sophronius' authorial notes about the oral transmission of the story among the monks at the monastery.

HILDEBERT OF LAVARDIN, 'THE LIFE OF BLESSED MARY OF EGYPT'[48]

Hildebert of Lavardin (1056–1134) is a notable medieval figure in two realms: ecclesiastical and literary. Educated at the cathedral school of Le Mans, he eventually became schoolmaster, archdeacon (1091), and, in a contested election, bishop of that city (1096–1125). He visited Rome and returned to Le Mans to oversee several building projects. He was elected archbishop of Tours in 1125 and remained in that post until his death. His survival in the church hierarchy is itself remarkable, for he had stormy relations with his king and other feudal lords, he endured a year's exile in England (lamented in a poem, *De exsilio suo*), and he was accused by other churchmen of scandalous behavior.

---

[48] Hildbert's *Life of Mary of Egypt* was published in 1708 by the Maurist Antony Beaugendre in his edition of Hildebert's works, and this edition was included by Migne in PL 171:967C–988B. It was also published by Daniel Papebroch in the *Acta Sanctorum*, April 1 (Antwerp: 1675). These editions have been superceded by Norbert Klaus Larsen's edition, *Hildeberti Cenomanensis Episcopi, Vita Beate Marie Egiptiace*, Corpus Christianorum Continuatio Mediaevalis, 209 (Turnhout: Brepols, 2004), on which this translation is based. Larsen distinguishes two main families among the ninety surviving manuscripts of Hildebert's work. He does so on the basis of the presence (a) or absence (b) of lines 347 (Canto 6, 'Offer hope to the chaste') and line 675 (Canto 10, 'If he, who alone governs all things, does not spurn you'). He conjectures that Hildebert himself added these lines. A smaller group of manuscripts inserts after verse 637 an addition of over three hundred fifty verses, which Larsen judges on stylistic grounds not to be the work of Hildebert. This addition is not translated here.

As an author, Hildebert's reputation has been exalted from his own day to ours. His extensive writings include epistles, hymns, epigrams, occasional verses, epitaphs, and two famous elegies on the city of Rome.[49] His prolific output and polished style won the admiration of contemporaries, and he received glowing praise from later medieval authors, including Peter of Blois and Lawrence of Durham. By modern scholars he is revered for his poetic verve, versification, and overall style; one literary historian refers to him as 'possibly the most important Latin poet of the later Middle Ages'.[50]

Early in the century after Hildebert's death, the anglo-latin poet Alexander Neckam paid tribute to him as part of a versified survey of European cities. In distinction 5 of *De laudibus divinae sapientiae* he wrote:

> Jam Cenomannis adest, cui magnus praeficit Hildebertus, flos cleri, pontificumque decus.
> Plurima festive scripsit dictamina, scripsit
> Sicut hyems laurum, Pergama flere nolo.

> Now there is Le Mans, which the great Hildebert presided over,
> The flower of the clergy and the glory of bishops.
> Wittily he wrote many letters; he wrote 'Just as winter
> The laurel' and 'I cannot weep over Troy'.

Embedded in these lines is a direct reference to Hildebert of Lavardin's *Life of Blessed Mary of Egypt*, for the words 'just as winter the laurel' *(sicut hyems laurum)* open Hilde-

---

[49] A. Brian Scott, ed., *Hildeberti Cenomanensis Episcopi Carmina minora* (Leipzig, 1969). A. Brian Scott, D. Baker, A.G. Rigg, 'The Biblical Epigrams of Hildebert of Le Mans: A Critical Edition', *Mediaeval Studies* 47 (1985) 272–316. See Peter von Moos, *Hildebert von Lavardin, 1056–1133: Humanitas an der schwelledes hofischen Zeitalters* (Stuttgart, 1969); A. Wilmart, 'Le florilège de Saint-Gatien: Contribution à l'étude des poèmes d'Hildebert et de Marbode', *Revue Bénédictine*, 48 (1936) 3–40, 147–181, 235–258.

[50] A. G. Rigg, *A History of Anglo-Latin Literature 1066–1422* (Cambridge: University Press, 1992) 64.

bert's life of Mary.[51] There is another, earlier testament to
it and its author as well. At some time before 1156, Bernard
of Cluny composed a long, lugubrious poem entitled *De
contemptu mundi* for his abbot, Peter the Venerable. In a
dedicatory prologue, Bernard acknowledged that he had
chosen for his work a highly challenging meter called *tri-
partiti dactylici caudati*, hexameter lines with both internal
and tailed rhyme. He noted that such a difficult form had
rarely been attempted, but he cited two 'most extraordi-
nary versifiers' who had done so successfully. Hildebert was
one of them, but even he, Bernard writes, composed only
four such verses in the life he wrote of 'that blessed sinner,
Mary—I am speaking of the Egyptian' (*illam beatam pec-
catricem Mariam—loquor Egyptiam*).[52] Those four verses
occur in Canto Nine:

> *Trina triennia, bina tetrennia sic abiere,*
> *Lenibus aspera, mitibus effera mista fuere.*
> *Sed nova vulnera Virgo puerpera, cum bene flevi,*
> *Tersit et abluit; inde salus fuit, inde quievi.*

> Thus, seventeen years elapsed; harsh times
> Were mixed with gentle ones, and savage times with
>   mild.
> But when I truly wept, the Virgin Mother wiped off
>   my new
> Wounds and washed them. Then there was salva-
>   tion; then I was at peace.

As a poet, Hildebert of Lavardin was imbued with the
classics. F. J. E. Raby, a foremost historian of medieval latin

[51] Hildebertus Cenomanensis, *Vita Beatae Mariae Aegyptiacae*; PL 171:1321–
1340. Konrad Kunze edited a middle dutch prose abbreviation and translation
of Hildebert's poem in his *Die Legende der heiligen Maria Aegyptiaca* (Berlin:
E. Schmidt, 1978) 95–103.

[52] Ronald E Pepin, introduction and translation, *Scorn for the World: Bernard
of Cluny's* De contemptu mundi (East Lansing: Colleagues [Michigan State
University Press], 1991) 8–9.

poetry, called him simply 'a master of classical Latin'.[53] Even
in works on religious subjects, he revealed his attachment
to the latin literature of antiquity. His *Life of Blessed Mary
of Egypt* is laced with echoes of the great roman writers
intermingled with sentiments drawn from Scripture. Thus,
the coming of evening *(venit hesperus)* and the haunts of
wild animals *(lustra ferarum)* and the welling up of tears
(lacrymis obortis) are expressed in vergilian terms. Ovid
supplies many phrases from his *Metamorphoses*, and his
amatory poems are represented as well. There are echoes of
Plautus, Horace, Lucan, and Juvenal. Even the elegiac poets
of love, Catullus and Tibullus, lend phrases to Hildebert.
In Canto Eleven he borrows Tibullus' *'Excubat ante fores'*
('May he keep watch before the gates') to advise an abbot.
These classical refrains are skillfully blended into a poem
whose themes, verses, and overall beauty of expression make
it an important work in the canon of latin poetry as well as
a valuable contribution to medieval hagiography.

Hildebert's poem follows the order of Sophronius' life and
presents its contents faithfully. There are some noteworthy
changes in emphasis and detail. Sometimes, Hildebert devel-
ops or makes explicit what is implied more subtly in Sophronius. For example, having said that Zosimas became a monk
at an early age, he employs in Canto One the *topos* of the
youth wise beyond his years with which Gregory the Great
described the young Saint Benedict. Hildebert portrays very
clearly that Zosimas, the austere monk, was tempted to pride
by enlarging the speech which told him to go to the monastery at the Jordan (Canto One). When Zosimas meets Mary
and they contend for each other's blessing, Mary argues that
Zosimas is her superior as man, monk, and priest (Canto
Three). Sophronius says that Mary lived on wild plants, but
was nourished by the Word of God; Hildebert elaborates:
Deprived of food, shelter and clothing, Mary was living proof

---

[53] F. J. E. Raby, *A History of Christian-Latin Poetry from the Beginnings to the
Close of the Middle Ages*, 2nd ed.(Oxford: Clarendon, 1953) 265.

that 'mankind does not live soundly by bread alone / Nor does a person withstand the winds by clothes or buildings alone: / God is sustenance for all; God is a whole garment for all' (Canto Nine). Mary had been supporting herself with what she made with needle and spindle, but she had also used them to make presents for her lovers (Canto Six).

Hildebert manifests some special interests in monasticism. In his description of the monastery along the Jordan River he emphasizes the equality of all the monks. The only official was the abbot and his way of life was exactly like that of all the other monks. He was a servant to the brothers, a school of justice, a whipping-rod of guilt, a cross to himself, a model to his flock—in Hildebert's own words, a *speculum monachorum*, a mirror for monks. Incredibly austere, isolated from the rest of society, the monks followed a regime that seems to have left them with considerable interior freedom (Canto One). Hildebert's description of the monastery reflects the ideals of the new reformed monasticism of late eleventh- and early twelfth-century Europe.[54] At the end of the account, Mary gives Zosimas a wordy admonition to deliver to the abbot, who is to nurture his monks in the observance of the rule (Canto Eleven). This contrasts sharply with the earlier description of the monastery, where all had seemed to be in good order and in which there was no mention of a rule (Canto One).[55]

Hildebert's low opinion of women and their bodies comes through in several places besides at Mary's reference to her threefold inferiority to Zosimas. In Canto Nine Mary describes her struggle as Eve against man, that is, flesh against spirit. Hildebert seems to think that female genitalia should be covered, not simply because of modesty, but because they

[54] Giles Constable, *The Reformation of the Twelfth Century* (New York: Cambridge University Press, 1996).

[55] Ronald Pepin, 'Monastic Themes in Hildebert of Lavardin's *Vita Beatae Mariae Aegyptiacae*', *Hommages à Carl Deroux, V: Christiansme et moyen-âge Néo-latin et survivance de la latinité*, ed. Pol Defosse (Bruxelles: Société d'Études latines de Bruxelles, 2003) 196–202.

are inherently shameful. Although he alludes to the glory of the risen body, he emphasizes the corruptibility of the body on earth. Mary's corpse is uncorrupted for a year, because it has been desiccated by asceticism. Hildebert does not include Mary's statement that since Zosimas has seen her bare body, she may as well lay bare her soul.[56]

Mary's relationship with Zosimas remains in Hildebert's what it was in Sophronius' account. On the two occasions when he leaves Mary to return to his monastery, Zosimas spends a year hoping and longing to see her again. When they were together, 'they rejoiced sincerely, the woman in the old man, / The man in the woman. The sum of their speech was God or moral lessons' (Canto Ten). When Zosimas returns to see her the third time, he discovers 'her flesh to be glorified, purer than melted gold', which 'lay covered as was proper for a woman'. He clings to her feet, weeps over them and kisses them, as the sinful woman had done to Jesus' feet in the gospel. The writing on the sand is a kind of riddle. In Hildebert's account Mary made the journey back into the desert in a moment, whereas it had taken Zosimas thirty days to reach her. Zosimas sets about preparing Mary's body for burial, something Mary did for herself in Sophronius' account. He closes her eyes. He did not have to wash her, because she was washed by tears and grace. Her body is uncorrupted after being exposed for a year to the elements and wild animals. In a strange reversal, Zosimas covers the body with his only garment, a battered tunic. Now Mary's body is clothed, and he is uncovered.

Hildebert frequently uses his poem to condemn drunkenness. In Canto Six, Mary says she was ruined by her sex, her youth, and drunkenness. In Canto Nine he emphasizes

---

[56] Larsen, *Vita*, 24–32, shows that in Hildebert's works and correspondence, the Virgin Mary, Saint Radegund, queen, widow, and nun, and Mary of Egypt, converted sinner, are the most prominent women. Zosimas stands as an exemplar for cenobitic monks and nuns, just as his Mary of Egypt could inspire both men and women converts. Hildebert wants to suggest that only very exceptional people can succeed in the eremitical life apart from church oversight.

again the role of drunkenness in Mary's wicked behavior. In Canto Two, when Zosimas brought her the Eucharist a year after their first meeting, she confessed, then received the chalice. Hildebert seems in Canto Nine to want again to contrast this pure drink with her earlier drunkenness.

Hildebert alters the story of Mary's conversion slightly. He does not say that her fellow passengers on the boat were pilgrims. He does say that Mary plumbed the depths of wantonness on the voyage. He claims she went to the church on the feast day because everyone else was going there. When she could not enter, she suddenly realized that it would not be right that the sacred place of Christ's redemption lie open to her, a harlot. She was torn; she sought to rise again, like Lazarus, there where Christ died and rose (Canto Eight). Canto Nine opens with her gazing at Mary's icon. 'While I gazed upon this, I was changed within, and I became another'. As she did in Sophronius' life, she refers to Mary as 'the Mother of our Father', for Christ 'is Father and Son at the same time'. She seeks to arise with the Virgin Mary as her intercessor, witness, and 'also the avenger' of her weakness. She had lived seventeen years in sin. After her conversion, she spends the next seventeen years struggling with temptations fed by the memory of her former sins. Finally she finds peace when her sins have been driven out by their contrasting virtues. With Blessed Mary's help, she has substituted hymns for jests, thirst for drunkenness, holy devotion for guilt, and punishment for pleasure.

Hildebert's account of Mary's life remains a story about divine mercy awaiting and abetting the conversion of sinners. Mary is convinced that she survived the sea voyage because 'the Lord Jesus, though offended, knew how to spare; / Though offended, he spared, and in sparing he showed how to return. / At length the Fount of Mercy freely showed me that, / Although angry he defers to punish our guilt, and / He is reluctant to strike, since he seeks to spare our faults' (Canto Seven). Even so, because the poem begins abruptly with the story of Zosimas' temptation to pride and ends

with his admonishing his fellow monks, the theme of mercy
is not as prominent as it will be in the Spanish poem of
Mary's life which will be discussed next. Moreover, Hildebert joins to the theme of divine mercy that of contempt
for the world. Contempt for the world is reinforced again
and again in the narrative and the dialogue of Hildebert's
Vita Beatae Mariae Aegyptiacae. The life of the spirit com-
mences with scorn for the world.

THE EARLY FRENCH VERSIONS

The Versions

In addition to the Latin lives, the Middle Ages produced a
very large number of vernacular accounts of Mary of Egypt.[57]
There are a number of french versions, from one of which
(designated as T) derives the spanish poem translated
below. Here it will be enough to raise some issues about
these french vernacular poems, especially T.

Several of the french versions of Mary's story change the
ordering and emphasis of the account. In this new arrange-
ment, which may be called 'type II', Mary overshadows Zosimas, who serves primarily to discover Mary and to tell her

---

[57] See those listed by Dembowski, *Vie*, 9–10, and the french versions he edits;
Kunze, *Legende*, edits german and latin versions from german-speaking regions,
and Poppe and Ross, *Legend*, contains references to many insular versions
(english, celtic, norse, anglo-norman). Mary of Egypt's popularity in medieval
Europe is also manifest in art. See Louis Réau, *Iconographie de l'art chrétien*
(Paris: Presses Universitaires de la France, 1958) 3/2: 884–888, and more recent
literature cited in Margaret Jennings, 'The Three Marys of Bourges', *Downside
Review*, 119/414 (January 2001) 35–50. In art Mary of Egypt was often associated with Mary Magdalene. She was most often represented as a hermit in the
desert, emaciated, either naked or covered with her own long hair. Whereas
Mary Magdalene was given the attribute of a jar of perfume, Mary of Egypt was
shown with three small loves of bread in her hand. Other medieval depictions
of Mary in stone and glass, show her offering her body to pay her passage to
Palestine, being repulsed by an angel at the entrance to the church in Jerusalem, imploring the Virgin Mary for forgiveness, washing her hair in the Jordan,
meeting Zosimas in the desert, and being buried by Zosimas and the lion.

story to others. All the narrative tensions are concentrated on the personal drama of Mary's sin, conversion, penance, and salvation. By contrast, in the versions which are more faithful to Sophronius (here called 'type I'), Zosimas is the primary figure. The main theme in type I is the spiritual development of Zosimas, who believes that he has reached the summit of perfection. He meets in Mary a humble simplicity that makes him fall in veneration at her feet and acknowledge his own sinfulness. In Sophronius' telling and subsequent type I versions, a monk meets a penitent; in T and other type II versions, a penitent meets a monk.

Dramatically, type I versions are at a disadvantage. When Mary comes to tell her life, both Zosimas and the reader know that she has converted. The reader is hearing her story as she told it to Zosimas, as he told it to the monks (and in some versions, they told it to Sophronius). Sophronius seems to have been trying to present what he took to be balanced views on monastic asceticism, the veneration of the true cross and of icons, the Eucharist, and devotion to the Virgin Mary. In type II versions, all these are mentioned, but only devotion to the Blessed Virgin Mary seems to receive strong emphasis. In type II versions, Mary of Egypt is described by the narrator in ways that would not be appropriate in her first person account in a type I version.[58]

---

[58] Dembowski, *Vie*, 21–23. Rutebeuf's version of the life of Mary of Egypt seems to rework T, just as the anonymous spanish poet did. Version T is a type II version, which makes Mary the central character. However, Rutebeuf also includes a lengthy passage (vv. 521–722) about the life and monastery of Zosimas. These lines he derived from O, a version of type I. Rutebeuf, who was concerned about monastic reform, may have added these lines because he felt they presented the most authentic version of this monastic tale. An edition of Rutebeuf's poem is included in Edmond Faral and Julia Bastin, *Oeuvres complètes de Rutebeuf* (Paris: Picard, 1969) 2:9–59. Brigitte Cazelles, *The Lady as Saint: A Collection of French Hagiographic Romances of the Thirteenth Century* (Philadelphia: University of Pennsylvania Press, 1991) 258–272, gives a summary and partial translation of Rutebeuf's version. Robertson, 119–123, agrees that Rutebeuf wished to restore the poem's monastic focus and to mute the atmosphere of courtly romance. He portrays Mary as a 'working girl', mixing learned diction with common, vernacular speech.

Two Interpretations

Brigitte Cazelles' interpretations of medieval french hagiography and particularly of T not only tell something about the french poem, but they suggest alternatives to the views presented below regarding the spanish life of Mary. She has argued that medieval french hagiography generally reserves sainthood for elite intermediaries between God and man. In these lives the saints imitate Christ in exceptional ways. They are intercessors and icons, and, at best, very distant models. Much of this vernacular hagiography was written in verse and transmitted in public performances. The verse form made it easier to remember, but it also gave a somewhat formulaic quality to the texts. Because it was written down, vernacular hagiography had the authority of a text, even though it was only heard orally. Although the hagiographic lives were written for all Christians, lives of women saints clearly had a particular relevance to female audiences. Yet, although the subjects of many of the lives were holy women, most of the authors were almost certainly men. In this body of hagiography a saint must be uncommon, but not improbable. The saints are at odds with the world, even though they are presented to the world. There is tension between the corporeal and the incorporeal, as saints attempt to achieve superhuman detachment from the temporal and sensory world. They are ascetics, hermits, pilgrims, and martyrs. They are shown to be edifying, impressive, and personable. The poet-hagiographers tended to be influenced by the styles and conventions of medieval romance. Hence, in these lives, the 'story evolves between a pious sermon and a folk song, for the pleasure of an audience which can confer upon its favorite hero a nostalgic or utopian victory over reality'.[59]

---

[59] Phyllis John and Brigitte Cazelles, *Le vain siècle guerpir: A Literary Approach to Sainthood through Old French Hagiography of the Twelfth Century*, University of North Carolina at Chapel Hill, Department of Romance Languages, no. 205 (Chapel Hill: North Carolina Studies in the Romance Languages and Literatures, 1979) 14–24, 192–193. Brigitte Cazelles, 'Modèle ou mirage: Marie

Because the stories of repentant sinners reveal human weakness and failure, their lives can seem to bridge the gap between saint and ordinary Christians, but Cazelles offers a caution regarding Mary of Egypt.

> The identification between Mary and the faithful is enhanced by her imperfection and her gradual growth in perfection. As a sinner, she incorporates and embraces the human condition. As a penitent, she offers a model of moral practice. By contrast, her sanctification is located beyond the ordinary, and the initial identification, if it exists, risks turning into a distancing.

In fact, Cazelles argues, Mary's sin is of epic proportions, her beauty unparalleled, and her willfulness overmastering. When her will meets an immovable barrier, she is suddenly converted. Her unique perversity is the foreshadowing of her superhuman holiness. She is transformed from anti-saint to icon of holiness.[60]

Cazelles believes that the achievements of the female saints are presented as almost inimitable conquests of 'woman's innate propensity to sin in the flesh'. Mary of Egypt's fasting and vigils resulted in the loss of her beauty 'and, consequently, her asset as a desirable prostitute, thus allowing her henceforth to lead a virtuous life'. Corporeality, specifically virginity and chastity, is the basis on which female saints gain sanctity, which in their case is usually discovered or made known posthumously. The vernacular lives emphasize transformations of women's bodies by disrobing, cross-dressing, or transformation. By disrobing,

---

l'Egyptienne', *The French Review*, 53 (1979) 13–22; Brigitte Cazelles, *Le Corps de sainteté d'après Jehan Bouche d'Or, Jehan Paulus, et quelques vies de xiie et xiiie siècles* (Geneva: Droz, 1982) 7–11. Cazelles, *The Lady as Saint*, 1–86. The text of the french original of T, ed. A. T. Baker, 'Vie de Sainte Marie l'Egyptienne', *Revue de Langues Romanes*, 61 (1916–1917) 283–379, is reprinted in Manuel Alvar, *Vida*, 2:113–148. Dembowski, *Vie*, 33–111, re-edits the poem.
[60] Cazelles, 'Modèle', 13–19; the quotation is translated from p. 15.

female saints are exposed to dangerous gazes, but they also
lay aside 'the artifices of female seductiveness'.[61]

Turning specifically to T, Cazelles notes the motif of pilgrimage or travel, which takes Mary to Jerusalem, to the
Judean Desert, and to a savage forest. These journeys widen
the distance between the convert and her former life, and
between the saint and the world. During her years in the
wilderness, Mary's appearance changes. She transcends her
former life and its temptations. The monks of the monastery also go to the desert wilderness to fast and meditate and
renew their contact with God. Zosimas joins them. After
Zosimas finishes a prayer for mercy, he looks toward the
east and sees a shape which may be a woman. Zosimas and
Mary become rivals in acknowledging the greatness of the
other. Because she is so isolated, so separated from others,
she needs Zosimas as an intermediary to inspire the monks
and others who will hear of her through them.[62]

Before fleeing to the desert, Mary had fled to the world,
to Alexandria, where she sought drink, food, and love with
the same intensity with which she was later to seek God.
After a while, she became bored. In the month of May she
wandered the harbor of Alexandria. She was enjoying the
sight of some pilgrims playing along the shore and impul-
sively decided to join them. When she offered her body
as her fare, the leader laughed. She appealed to the young
men's charity, and they endorsed her request— perhaps out
of very mixed motives, as her ready conquest of all of them
during the voyage suggests. In Jerusalem, Mary seems to
try to find company in crowds, in the arms of men, even
in processions. So it is that she is very distraught when she
cannot enter the church. She realizes the extent of her sin
and turns to the Virgin Mary for help, and that act begins
the next stage of her pilgrimage. Mary is credibly portrayed

[61] Cazelles, *The Lady*, 41–61.
[62] Johnson and Cazelles, *Le vain siècle*, 99–103.

as a strong-willed, resourceful, insecure, restless woman of intense longings who was transformed by repentance.[63]

Duncan Robertson, who regards T as a hagiographical masterpiece, provides another perspective on this french version of the Life of Mary of Egypt. In Robertson's estimation, the poet who wrote T possessed a good knowledge of the desert monks of the early Church, of christian doctrine, and of vernacular court romances, all of which helped him to reinterpret the latin version from which he worked. The poet's prologue emphasizes that the legend is an *exemplum* of repentance. No sin is unforgivable, except despair itself. God grants forgiveness 'through faith and confession' to all who do penance (lines 15–19). Making repentance his theme helps the poet move the story of Mary of Egypt into a wider, non-monastic context.[64]

By beginning with a third-person narrative about Mary, the poet is free to describe her beauty and virtues, and he increases the drama by switching his attention from Mary to Zosimas, then bringing the two together. He adds a description of her youthful beauty, which he can then contrast with a description of her as she was just before her death. When she was young, her neck was as white as ermine, her breasts no smaller than apples, and her bosom white as the hawthorn flower (lines 175–180). By the time Zosimas met her, it was Mary's hair which was white as ermine, while her bosom was flat as a glove and black like the bark of the hawthorn (ll. 630–644).[65]

[63] Johnson and Cazelles, *Le vain siècle*, 152–158.

[64] Robertson, 106–107. References to T will be given in the text in parentheses according to the line numbers in the edition in Dembrowski, *Vie*, 33–66.

[65] The description of Mary of Egypt's beauty with which she seduces her lovers reminds Robertson of a scene in the story of Saint Pelagia. Bishop Nonnus is at a meeting of bishops, when Pelagia flounces by decked with jewels. When the other bishops turned their eyes away, Nonnus asked: 'Are you not delighted at such beauty?' He contrasted Pelagia's care for the beauty of her body with the indifference of Christians toward the beauty of their souls. Nonnus later baptized Pelagia (Robertson, 97–98, 107–109). For this story about Pelagia, see Sebastian Brock and Susan Ashbrook Harvey, *Holy Women of the Syrian Orient*, 2nd ed. (Berkeley: University of California Press, 1998) 42–51; Ward, *Harlots*, 67–71.

The french poet gives a frank description of Mary's love-making with the pilgrims on the boat, but at the same time he makes no excuses for her. She acts out of lust alone; in her actions there is no hint of any affection, but neither is there any greed. She is unmoved when her suitors kill or wound each other.[66] Her unbridled desire and self-abandonment before her conversion mirror in reverse her self-abnegation as a penitent. She is the same passionate lover throughout the story. When Mary fled her family at the age of twelve, she rejected not only her kin, but the rich husband her mother had promised her if she reformed. Her abandonment of her family for lust is a perverse parody of saints who left behind family, marriage and homeland to seek God alone.[67]

Having plumbed the depths of wickedness, Mary undergoes a profound reversal. She confesses 'I am poor and proud, and lustful with my body' (ll. 473–474). Her change of heart is made possible by the Blessed Virgin, and to her Mary of Egypt addresses a prayer in which she quotes the angel's address *(Ave Maria)* and uses some of the traditional metaphors of marian devotion, thereby fashioning a prayer that is shared by the fledgling saint and the reader (ll. 417–421, 457–464).[68]

At Mary's first meeting with Zosimas, her blackened body is covered by her long white hair, but revealed when the wind catches her hair (ll. 846–848).[69] She has revealed herself to God, who has revealed her to Zosimas. She teases him: 'Good, dear father, why are you afraid. Why are you afraid of a woman?' (ll. 993–995) Later, when she agrees to tell him her story, she says: 'Since you have seen me nude, my life shall be revealed to you'

[66] A similar story about her lovers fighting over her occurs in the story of Thaïs. See Robertson, 96, 110.

[67] Robertson, 110–111.

[68] Robertson, 111–113.

[69] Mary's long hair is a detail not found in Sophronius or in Paul the Deacon, who describe her hair as sparse and reaching only to her neck. Heron (40–41) comments on this detail, which appears in *The Old English Life of Saint Mary of Egypt* and which she thinks may derive from the iconography of Mary Magdalene. Saint Agnes' hair grew to cover her; see Donovan, 49, 127.

(ll. 1014–1018). After hearing her story, Zosimas would like to stay with her, but she gently refuses and tells him: 'God has shown me to you; by you I wish to be hidden' (ll. 1045–1046). When Zosimas returns a year after their first meeting and brings her communion, Mary falls at his feet and begs him to bless her. When she arises, he kisses her in true friendship. He recites the creed and the Lord's Prayer for her. 'They gaze at each other continuously' (ll. 1173–1188).[70] This addition of an element of chaste eroticism is one way in which the french poet adapts Sophronius' tale to a new audience of aristocratic women. Mary of Egypt, not Zosimas, is the primary seeker. She, like the Blessed Virgin, represents the possibility of sanctity for anyone. Zosimas, the priest, and the Blessed Virgin who serves as the guarantor (*fidejussor*)[71] of Mary's continuing conversion, are joint mediators between God and the repentant Mary and the audience of the poem.[72]

---

[70] The erotic element in Zosimas' attachment to Mary of Egypt has often been remarked. See, for example, Magennis, 5–6; Robertson, 114–115.

[71] This is the word used in Paul the Deacon's translation of Mary of Egypt's prayer before the icon (ed. Magennis, line 512) and is used also used to refer to the person who stands as guarantor for Pelagia's continuing conversion; see Robertson, 97, 117.

[72] Robertson, 114–118. Robertson edits a prayer which an unknown scribe (he hypothesizes she was a nun) addressed to Mary Magdalene and through her to the Blessed Virgin, and appended to MS Paris, Bibliothèque Nationale, fonds français 23112, a collection of hagiographical works which includes the text which served as the basis for Drembowski's edition of T. The poem contains several echoes of the Mary of Egypt's prayers in T. Robertson (264) comments: 'The poem makes a statement of participation in the virtual community of religious, literary women who acknowledged the Virgin as their ultimate patron; it expresses–rather eloquently, I find–the personal, interactive relationship which linked readers and writers of saints' lives to the heroes and heroines of the legendary tradition.' In a paper delivered at the Medieval Congress in Kalamazoo, 9 May 2003, 'Telling Infromation in Old French Lives', Amy Ogden notes that the prayers attributed to Mary of Egypt in T and similar prayers in other twelfth-century french saints' lives summarize the history of salvation. The reiteration of the familar biblical story is meant to lead the reader to wisdom by eliciting a response in feeling and action and to validate the truth of the narrative. Temptation in salvation history reflects Mary of Egypt's own tempting and being tempted, and the story of salvation shows the availability of divine mercy and the importance of the Blessed Virgin as intercessor. See also, Donovan, 8–9.

REPENTANCE AND CONTRITION

The doctrine of repentance underwent a rapid evolution in the twelfth century. In the previous centuries, primarily through the work of monks from the british isles, the use of penitential tariffs had spread across Europe. Whatever the shortcomings of the penitentials and their tariffs for various sins, they did provide a form of penance which could be repeated, which took into account circumstances of the sinner and his sin, and which inculcated a sense of personal responsibility.

Meanwhile, from its early days monasticism had emphasized the need for compunction and tears. In the tenth century monastic preachers like Saint Romuald and Saint Peter Damian preached conversion, flight from the world, and tearful repentance to people—both noteworthy and obscure—who lived beyond the cloister. Sometimes repentance was expressed in acts of penitence, which might have been as onerous as going on a crusade or a pilgrimage, or as simple as almsgiving or prayers.

At the same time, the Gregorian Reform was emphasizing the role of the priest in sacramental life. The priest's role in the forgiveness of sins became accentuated. His intercession could be decisive in the penitent's effort to receive pardon. Tears were a sign that the penitent deserved to be absolved. As a result, confession to lay persons declined, though people continued to confess to non-ordained monks and hermits throughout the twelfth century.[73]

The twelfth century saw the development of a doctrine of repentance called contritionism. According to this doctrine

> the remission of sins occurs in the following manner: the sinner agrees to an infusion of divine grace, which arouses in him tears of repentance. These tears are the visible sign of a divine pardon already

[73] Jean-Charles Payen, *Le motif du repentir dans la littérature française médiévale (des Origines à 1230)* (Geneva: Droz, 1967) 9–53.

granted, and this 'true contrition' (the term 'perfect contrition' only appeared later) immediately lifts the sanction of eternal punishment. It remains for the sinner to lift the sanction of limited punishment which he needs to undergo in reparation for his fault. Earthly penance removes the threat of a more severe expiation after death. On the other hand, because of his state of sin, the sinner is separated from the visible church with which he can only be reconciled through priestly absolution.[74]

Contritionism arose in part from the tearful and devout compunction cultivated in monastic circles. Anselm of Canterbury (c. 1033–1109) and Ivo of Chartres (c. 1040–1115) contributed to the theory, in part by emphasizing the importance of intention in sin and repentance. Abelard (1079–1142/3), Hugh of Saint Victor (†1142), Peter Lombard (c. 1100–1160), and others developed the theory. According to Hugh of Saint Victor, consent to some evil action is decisive in culpability, even if the actual performance of the evil act does not follow. Similarly, sincere contrition is necessary to repentance, but the sinner must also confess to a priest. As contrition gives interior release from sin, so external penance releases one from the evil act. Richard of Saint Victor (†1173) taught that the role of the priest is not to bring the sinner back to life, but to unbind him—that is, to mitigate his punishment. In the estimate of Jean-Charles Payen, the several vernacular verse lives of Saint Mary of Egypt written in the twelfth and thirteenth centuries—including that of the renowned thirteenth-century french poet Rutebeuf—were contritionist in their conception of repentance.[75] Contritionism is a motif in the Spanish life of Mary of Egypt also.

---

[74] Payen, *Motif,* 54.
[75] Payen, *Motif,* 54–75, 104. According to Payen (76–84), contritionism seems to have declined in part because of the rise of frequent confession. Frequent

MARY OF EGYPT AND THE ROLES OF WOMEN

Mary of Egypt is neither of the nobility, nor wife, nor mother, nor virgin, nor educated, nor enclosed in a monastery, nor exactly a prostitute. From the time of Sophronius to the twelfth-century and beyond, Mary of Egypt is a strong-willed, passionate, non-conforming and autonomous woman. She breaks with her parents when she is twelve, rejecting her family of birth and the prospect of marriage to a rich husband. She never sees her family again. Rather than live off her lovers, she supports herself by spinning during the time she lives in debauchery in Alexandria. She trades her favors for the trip to Jerusalem, but, even so, she pays her own way. Before she gets on the boat she throws away her spindle or distaff, thereby distancing herself from her livelihood and from a distinctly and almost universal feminine activity (Sophronius 18–20).[76] At the door to the church the hitherto irresistible force of her will runs headlong into a supernatural wall. Stopped in her tracks, she promises the Blessed Virgin to obey her, if only she is allowed into the church. She then goes to the desert where she lives as a hermit, overcoming her lustful habits and living off the land. Although she has the deepest respect for Zosimas' status as a priest and desires to receive the Eucharist, she has lived alone for over forty-five years,

---

confession, though it encouraged regular self-examination, required a more routine, less intense sense of contrition. Also, in the understanding and practice of the sacrament itself, the role of the priest increased while the role of the penitent was reduced. Thirteenth-century theologians developed a theology of penitence which replaced contritionism. According to Saint Thomas Aquinas (1225–1274), penance is both a virtue and a sacrament. Contrition, which disposes the sinner to repentance, the confession itself, and the works of satisfaction which follow are informed by the grace conferred by the absolution pronounced by the priest.

[76] Karen Winstead, *Virgin Martyrs: Legends of Sainthood in Late Medieval England* (Ithaca, New York: Cornell University Press, 1997) 108, notes that this detail of Mary's life appears in the *South English Legendary*, 'where Mary of Egypt is represented as a working woman who entices men to sin for the sheer fun of it; Mary did not charge for her services, for . . . she earned her living by spinning and sewing'.

praying by herself, without benefit of clergy or sacraments, with the Blessed Virgin as her guarantor and guide. Having rejected the secular world's expectations for women, Mary carves out her own niche in the christian world by becoming a contemplative hermit. The medieval women and men must have learned from her story not only the wideness of God's mercy, but the variety of paths, some quite circuitous, by which they could come to God, if only they loved as passionately and willed as strongly as Mary of Egypt did.[77]

THE ANONYMOUS SPANISH POETIC LIFE (*VIDA*)

The story of Mary of Egypt was popular in Spain. There are many spanish versions. These include the poem discussed and translated below (here referred to as the *Vida*),[78] a related prose life *(Estoria)*, a translation of Paul the Deacon's latin version, and four translations of the brief life of Mary of Egypt in the *Legenda aurea*.[79] The spanish poet of the *Vida* is a translator. For the most part he follows his french original (T, a type II version). Sometimes he is inaccurate and sometimes he is creative. He adds little touches of humanity and

[77] See, for example, Donovan, 11–15, 121–134; Heron.

[78] There have been a number of editions of this spanish poem. The two most recent are María S. de Andrés Castellanos, *La Vida de Santa María Egipçiaca, traducida por un juglar anónimo hacia 1215* (Madrid: Anejos del Boletín de la Real Academia Española, 1964), and Alvar, *Vida*. Alvar's edition includes a facsimile of the manuscript containing the poetic and prose versions that he edits, a paleographic edition of the poem, and critical editions of the poem and the prose version. It is his critical edition of the poem which is translated here.

[79] The spanish versions of Paul the Deacon and the *Legenda aurea* are edited by B. Russell Thompson and John K. Walsh, *La Vida de Santa María Egipçiaca: A Fourteenth-Century Translation of a Work by Paul the Deacon* (Exeter: University of Exeter, 1977). The prose life was edited by Roger M. Walker, *Estoria de Santa María Egipçiaca* (Exeter: University of Exeter, 1972), and by Alvar, *Vida*, 2:151–167. Alvar discusses this prose text in *Vida*, 1: 113–124. He concludes that the french poem, which was translated into the spanish poem now translated here, also was the basis for a french prose text which in turn was translated into the spanish prose *Estoria*.

realism to the story he is translating and so makes it more
accessible to his spanish audience. He weds the concerns and
styles of *juglar* (minstrel) and cleric as he seeks to entertain
and to instruct. The *Vida* contains about the same number
of words as Sophronius' original Greek version and is about
90 lines shorter than the French original. The abbrevia-
tions it makes occur mostly in the last quarter of the french
poem.[80] The spanish poet made his translation in the first
part of the thirteenth century, within a half century of the
composition of its french exemplar. Sometimes the poet uses
the spanish honorific *Don* for Zosimas or another monk.[81]
In what follows, references to the paragraphs of Sophronius'
life are indicated by arabic numerals; references to the *Vida*
are indicated by roman numerals.

The *Vida* begins with an author's introduction, which
echoes that of Sophronius (i;1). Then it adds two sections
(ii–iii) not in Sophronius, which emphasize the mercy of
God and the need for repentance before death and judgment overtake one. These include a rather theological discussion of the nature of sin. The *Vida* returns to the theme
of God's judgment near the end (xxxi). In contrast to these
warnings, the poet notes that while Mary was sinning lustily
on the pilgrimage ship during a dangerous storm, she gave
no thought to the possibility and consequences of sudden
death (viii).

The *Vida*, following its type II french exemplar, begins its
narrative with the story of Mary's life (iv-xvi, 18–30), which
is told in the third person. Describing her wanton youth,
the poet includes a poignant dialogue between her and her
mother that is not in Sophronius' account (iv, 18). The
author implies that Mary's family was noble, but somewhat
impoverished. By the time of this dialogue, Mary's father
had given up on her. The poet then tells the story of Mary's

---

[80] Alvar, *Vida*, 1:109–112; 31–40. Castellanos, *Vida*, 76–80.
[81] Alvar, *Vida*, 91. One might have translated *don* with the monastic title
'dom'.

sinful life and of her conversion. After that, he leaves her for a while to describe at some length the monastery where Zosimas lived. This leads him to a description of the monks' lenten practice of going out alone into the desert (xviii, 5–8). He does not mention Zosimas' earlier monastic experience (2–4), but gives the impression that Zosimas had always been a monk at the monastery by the Jordan River. There follow Zosimas' initial meeting with Mary (xix–xxiv, 9–17), their second meeting (xxvi–xxvii, 33–36), Mary's burial (xxix, 37–40), Zosimas' return to the monastery (xxx, 41), and a final exhortation (xxxi).

In the consideration of motifs and ideas which follows, the main point of comparison is between the Vida and the *Life of Mary of Egypt* by Sophronius outlined above. Only occasionally will the differences between the *Vida* and its french source (T) be discussed. The interpretations of the french poem that were presented above suggest ways of reading the *Vida* that differ from what is presented below.

Conversion, Contrition and Sacraments

Early in the poem, the spanish poet gives inklings of Mary's upcoming, wholehearted conversion. There are at least three factors leading to her conversion: growing restlessness and dissatisfaction with her way of life; her very strong will; and her relationships with others.

Toward the end of her years in Alexandria, Mary enters a transitional period in which her old ways and the new life toward which she is being drawn are mixed together. Thus, in arranging for her passage to Jerusalem, Mary sounds very religious as she asks for alms for God's sake, even though she is ready to play the prostitute to pay for her passage (vii). God protected her during her voyage because he was preparing her heart for conversion (viii, 21). She also is sad and disconsolate when she finds herself friendless and homeless in Jerusalem, so she returns to her old ways with a vengeance (ix), though it seems that she already knows in her heart that 'the pleasure of this life / All turns to great sadness' (xxvii).

She was, as we noted earlier, a very willful person who would not be thwarted once she had set her mind on something. Her willfulness made her the despair of her parents; she 'abandoned her family / In order to do what she wanted' (iv). Later, when she decided to leave Alexandria for Jerusalem, she allowed nothing to stand in her way. When she was thwarted in her desire to enter the church, not only did she recognize her sinfulness, but she also begged Mary to help her fulfill her desire to enter (ix). Then she applied her indomitable will to doing what she had promised the Virgin Mary she would do.

One might say that in spite of, or perhaps because of, all her lovers, Mary was haunted by a need to belong, to connect with someone, even though she acted 'like a thief / Who wanted no companion' (v). The spanish poet adds an entertaining, if appalling, twist to the description of Mary's wild life in Alexandria. As her admirers fight over her, Mary is supremely indifferent to the injuries they inflict on each other. She has many admirers, so the death of one or two of them in a duel is of no consequence. Although, like Sophronius, the *Vida* presents her as driven by enormous sexual appetites, it also shows her toying with her lovers in a rather aloof and arrogant way (v).[82] By the time she reached Jerusalem, her isolation was complete. 'She knew neither man nor woman', she was 'weeping and confused' (ix). She found a friend and intercessor in the Virgin Mary, and applied her will to following where her pact with the Virgin Mary led her.

---

[82] The life of another converted prostitute, Thaïs, says that 'quarrels arose among her lovers and often the doorstep of this girl's house was soaked in the blood of young men' (Ward, *Harlots*, 83). Stevenson, 'Holy Sinner', 26–28, discusses how the portrait of Mary reflects the then reigning (male) views of female sexuality. She thinks that Zosimas' discovery that this despised non-person was a great saint would have been a shocking twist to the prevailing sensibilities of Sophronius' time.

In the end, her conversion to God brings her a true friend, the monk Zosimas.

Both Sophronius and the spanish poet teach that human repentance is a response to the mercy of God. Both say that Mary was pardoned as soon as she repented in her heart (xi [end], 24). The spanish author, following his french exemplar, has Mary make a complete, candid, and heartfelt confession of her sins to Sophronius the priest (xxiii).[83] The result is that to Mary's other exemplary functions, the spanish poet adds that of a model of how to make a proper confession. He writes (ii) that there is no sin

> That God will not pardon
> Through penitence and confession;
> To anyone who repents from the heart
> God gives pardon.
> Those who accept penance. . . .

The author does not explicitly mention that she receives absolution after she has finished making her full confession. Zosimas can only admire her holiness and diffidently ask her to arise. This theology of repentance is contritionist.

The two basic christian sacraments of Baptism and Eucharist figure in the story. When Zosimas is afraid that Mary may be some sort of devilish illusion, Mary assures him that she is a Christian baptized in infancy (xxiii). After she has converted, she goes to the monastery on the banks of the river and washes in the sacred waters (xiii), but she does not receive the Body and Blood of her Lord (cf. 26).[84] When she meets Zosimas, she asks him to bring her consecrated bread and wine, so that she may receive communion in the Body

---

[83] The theology and practice of confession were much discussed in the twelfth and thirteenth centuries(see above, n. 75). In his Sermon 14, for example, Achard of Saint Victor explains that to be perfect a confession should be voluntary, candid, and sincere (*voluntaria, nuda, munda*); (*Sermons inédits*, ed. Jean Châtillon [Paris: Vrin, 1970] 180–186). The confession which Zosimas elicits from Mary is all of these.

[84] Castellaños, *Vida*, 77.

and Blood of Christ (xxiv, 32). In the event, that communion is her *viaticum*. In the spanish poem, Zosimas (whom Mary calls '*misacantano*' ['mass-singer']) offers a brief theology of the Eucharist as he gives her communion (xxvi). These references to the theology of the Eucharist seem to reflect the theological concerns which led the Fourth Lateran Council to pronounce authoritatively on the transubstantiation of bread and wine into the Body and Blood of Christ.[85] Mary, who lived for so long on three small loaves of bread, is even more abstemious in receiving the Eucharist.

SEXUAL BODIES AND SPIRITUAL FRIENDS

The spanish poet, following—though not slavishly—his french exemplar, adds to Sophronius' text two contrasting portraits of Mary of Egypt. One describes her youthful physical beauty and the fancy clothes she wore in her worldly years (vi);[86] the other describes her appearance when Zosimas met her after she had spent forty-seven years in the desert (xv). In the first description of Mary in the bloom of youth, the author contrasts her white skin with her dark hair and eyes and her rosy cheeks.[87] In the latter portrait, he revisits each facet of her former beauty from top to bottom. Her hair, ears, eyes, mouth, breasts, arms, nails, stomach, and feet are now weather-beaten and without charm. She has lost her healthy

---

[85] Carmen Wyatt-Hayes, *Representations of Holiness in Some Spanish Hagiographical Works: The Thirteenth through the Seventeenth Centuries* (Unpublished doctoral dissertation, Stanford University, 1983) 100.

[86] Mary's beauty, her clothes, her noble lineage, her courtesy, are all elements which connect her with the heroines of chivalric romance. Mary embarks for Jerusalem in May, the conventional time for new love (Wyatt-Hayes, 101–102). The spanish poet adds two references to Mary carrying her birds, one of which sang. These additions reflect the lyric tradition and perhaps provençal influence. On the birds see Castellaños, *Vida*, 76; Wyatt-Hayes, *Representations*, 108–109.

[87] The spanish poet adds some personal touches to his translation of the portraits of Mary in the french exemplar; see Alvar, *Vida*, 1:33–37. In his second portrait he mentions that she had had red hair.

color and is burned dark by the sun and frost and shrunken from years of fasting and hardship. Unlike Saint Antony,[88] she did not look healthy after her years of solitary asceticism. In her old age she is like the bride of the Canticle, black of body. Like the bride she is also beautiful, but only in her heart. There is, however, a way in which her virtue is made visible. In both Sophronius and the spanish poem, Mary's wrinkled, darkened body is also preternaturally transformed: her body radiates light (xxiv); she lives on almost no food (xvi, 30); after seventeen years of struggle her body becomes fully attuned to her faith (xvi, 28-30); she can walk on water (xxvi, 35) and levitate (xxii, 15) The ascetical humiliation of her body brought her the humility of heart that Zosimas was seeking, while the purity of her heart prepared for the transformation of her body.[89] Sophronius had the pilgrims going to Jerusalem for the Feast of the Holy Cross. The *Vida* changes that to the Feast of the Ascension (vii, 22), perhaps because the feast is the occasion of her ascent from a life of bodily dissipation to one of ethereal freedom.

In the accounts of both Sophronius and the spanish poet, Mary's nudity is a prominent theme. This emphasis seems to intend no reference to the primordial state of Adam and Eve before their sin.[90] Mary's nudity in the desert exposes her to the elements, so that she is bleached and burned by both frost and cold (xv). Sophronius says her hair was short; the *Vida* says it had grown very long (xix, 10). Neither she nor Zosimas is comfortable with her nudity. She will not turn toward him until he tosses her a cloak which she can wrap around her (xx, 12–13). These two holy people have not reached a state of sexless indifference. Even though Mary's body is old and emaciated, the implication is that it could be

---

[88] Athanasius, *The Life of Saint Antony*, 93; translated Robert T. Meyer (New York: Paulist, 1978] 96–97; translated Tim Vivian, *The Life of Antony. The Coptic Life and The Greek Life* (Kalamazoo: Cistercian, 2003) 257.

[89] Posa, 'Mary and Zossima', 15–18.

[90] See, for example, *La Sostanza dell' Effimero: gli abiti degli ordini religiosi in Occidente*, ed. Giancarlo Rocca (Rome: Paoline, 2000) 35, 127.

a source of temptation to Zosimas. The eroticism with which the initial meeting and their brief and quickly developing relationship is charged is, however, subsumed into mutual respect and love that reverence the holiness of the other.

In both texts, Mary says that since Zosimas has seen her bare body, she lays bare to him the story of her life (xxiii, 17). She is willing to tell her whole life story because she trusts Zosimas. He has seen her naked by accident and has not taken advantage of her, but shown her great respect. In their contests of humility, in which each wants the other's blessing, Zosimas hugs her feet. She lifts him up, and later, after he has brought her communion, he in turn helps her up. The spanish text has them refer to each other as 'Lady' and 'Sir', but in it they also call each other 'friend'. Their friendship was founded on the friendship each had with God. When they meet a second time, they exchange a liturgically sanctioned kiss (xxvi, 35). Zosimas is so in awe of Mary's holiness that he would like to stay with her, but she sends him back (xxiv, 36). Even when Mary is dead, Zosimas will touch no part of her but her feet.

One could interpret this poem as misogynistic, or at least as reflecting the point of view of a monk who could see in women nothing more than a source of temptation. In such a reading, Mary's youthful beauty was nothing more than a temptation, or rather, a means Mary could use to satisfy her insatiable, female lusts.[91] She could become a desert saint only by a long ascetical regime that shriveled her female body. Yet such a reading does not seem to do justice to the *Vida*. The message of this story is not that the female body or its beauty or its pleasures are evil. In the added introductory sections, the spanish poet declares: 'Our Lord gave her beauty' (ii). 'Sin is not a created being / But a disturbance arising in nature' (iii). In fact, even after her long sojourn in

[91] See the discussion above of Brigitte Cazelles' analysis of T for some intimations of such an interpretation, and, for a more general discussion, Anne Marie Dalton, 'The Challenge of Violence: Toward a Theology of Women's Bodies', *Toronto Journal of Theology*, 16/2 (2000) 235–250.

the desert, Mary is still recognizably female. There is erotic energy in her meeting with Zosimas, but it arises not from some inherent female lust, but from the fact that Zosimas is looking upon her naked body. He, however, regards her with deep reverence, and this leads her to trust him and lay bare her life to him. At the end, Mary says to God: 'I commend my body and soul to you' (xxviii). Then she composes herself reverently on the ground and dies. With great tenderness, Zosimas and the lion bury her body (xxix) in a place more precious than balsam (xxviii).

THE COMMUNION OF SAINTS

The accounts of Mary of Egypt's life have a geographical frame. The monastery of Saint John is situated on the west bank of the Jordan. When directions are given, it is the east and the right that are mentioned (xiv, xix, xxix, 10, 15). Across the river is the desert, which in the spanish text is mountainous. Depending on one's perspective, the promised land is on either side of the river. The far, deserted side is the place of personal charism and heroic holiness represented by Mary. There Mary finds God in a particularly intimate and personal way. Yet this desert is also an inhospitable and harsh place. The near side of the river is the place of the institutional Church, the liturgy, and the community of exemplary monks, represented by Zosimas. Mary and Zosimas vie in asking for blessings and prayers from the other. That is the only rivalry that should occur between institution and charism.[92] Mary of Egypt admonishes the abbot through Zosimas (xxiii, xxxi, 32, 40); his community remembers her.

In Sophronius' account, Mary of Egypt is a model for desert anchorites, while Zosimas and the monks of Saint John are models of desert cenobites. The *Vida* adds touches

---

[92] Jane Stevenson makes similar observations in 'Holy Sinner', 22–23, citing tensions in the church of Sophronius' time.

that evoke the monastic observance with which the author was familiar. In particular, the *Vida* mentions the importance of fidelity to the liturgy of the hours (xvii). It is also possible to detect the same criticism of some less stringent forms of benedictine cenobitism which appeared in Hildebert of Lavardin. Thus, both Sophronius and the spanish poet emphasize the desert monks' poverty (5, xvii), but the latter may do so with an edge of criticism aimed at monks of his time.[93] When Mary is trying to get the pilgrims to take her with them, she says she has only one coin: 'here is all my treasure / my silver and gold' (vii). She seems to be referring to her body as much as to any coin. In the spanish version, her greed or need for money looms larger in her wicked conduct than it does in either Sophronius or the french poem. Her mother grieves that Mary may be lost for lack of a dowry (iv). Mary had no interests but spending and consuming (iv). She gave herself to those with money. She noticed that the pilgrim ship had rich men on board (vii). When she finally turned to God, she found in him all her treasure, just as the Blessed Virgin did (xi). In the process Mary of Egypt herself became the Lord's hidden treasure, more precious than gold (37). This concern with money and poverty seems to reflect the same interests that inspired the mendicant movement of the time, if not direct mendicant influence.[94] There may also be an endorsement of the new religious movements of the twelfth- and thirteenth-century—such as the Franciscans—which abandoned the stability of place envisaged by the Rule of Benedict. Both Mary and Zosimas are mobile pilgrims. The monastic community on the Jordan River incorporates movement and solitude into its yearly round, thereby synthesizing stability and pilgrimage, community and eremitical living.[95]

---

[93] For example, the spanish poet adds that no one would give a ripe apple for Zosimas' tunic, though Zosimas would not take a horse in exchange for it (xix).

[94] Wyatt-Hayes, *Representations*, 112–114.

[95] On this last point, see Wyatt-Hayes, *Representations*, 103–104.

The story of Mary of Egypt is a saint's life, and it is suffused with a sense of the communion of saints. One theme in Sophronius' text and the *Vida* is the place of Blessed Mary, with whom Mary of Egypt shares a name and physical comeliness, though they led very different lives. Sophronius makes much of the icon of Mary which was on display at the Church of the Holy Sepulcher. He presents Mary as Mother of God, ever-virgin, who serves as her egyptian namesake's guarantor and guide. The spanish poet presents Mary as Virgin Queen of Heaven.[96] When Mary of Egypt entreats Mary's icon, she gives a summary of the story and theology of both Mary and her Son (24–26, 28, xi–xiv).[97]

Mary of Egypt is presented as a model of the process of conversion which leads from sin, through contrition and penance, to a new life. As Cazelles noted regarding the french life of Mary of Egypt, there is little else in Mary's story that the ordinary person can imitate. Her wickedness and holiness are so superhuman that few would need to be warned away from her excesses, for no one would aspire to her life of penitence. She is most accessible in her repentance and conversion, and the subsequent seventeen years of struggle against sin do reflect the experience of ordinary monks and other Christians.

In her time of greatest need, Mary of Egypt found an intercessor and guarantor in Mary, the Mother of God and Queen of Heaven. Similarly, the poet adds a final exhortation urging that his readers, like the monks of Zosimas' monastery, not only amend their lives according to Mary of Egypt's example, but also

> . . . entreat this Mary
> Every night and day

---

[96] On the veneration of Mary as Queen of Heaven, which flourished in the twelfth century, see Penny Shine Gold, *The Lady and the Virgin: Image, Attitude, and Experience in Twelfth-Century France* (Chicago: University of Chicago Press, 1985) 51–68.

[97] Jennings, 'The Three Marys', 45–46; Stevenson, 'Holy Sinner', 46.

that she entreat the Creator
With whom she shares great love
That we may perform such service
That on the day of judgment
we will not fall into condemnation.

Then, turning his attention from Mary to her Creator he exclaims:

May He give us a great share
In everlasting life.[98]

[98] Wyatt-Hayes, *Representations*, 116–120.

FLODOARD
OF REIMS

ON THE TRIUMPHS OF CHRIST
AND THE SAINTS OF PALESTINE

BOOK ONE, CHAPTER FOUR

ON MARY THE EGYPTIAN AND ZOSIMAS

. . . Others dwelt in Palestine, and they
were men distinguished
For virtues, men who followed the strait path,
Excellent men who sought the heights of Heaven.
Some of them pleased God when they went
into the wilderness,
But others pleased him equally when they
gathered in fraternal
Peace and stayed under the law of heaven in monasteries.
Of these monasteries the banks of the Jordan
formerly held one
Where they say the law thrived according to the time,
For the battle was fought in common for almost a year
Before the day when at length the lenten fasts begin
To be borne in the accustomed way. Then, while all
As hermits sought out desolate places, they
took up the individual
Struggles of life, but when the feast of Easter returned, they
Rushed back so that they could praise the
Lord of Peace together.

Led by direction from above, Zosimas
entered this monastery.
Although each one fights the battle for Christ, he thought
That he had surpassed the rest in faithful service.
Coming here therefore, and made a disciple at last
In this struggle, he intended to take up the rule.
While he wandered in the wilderness
at the time mentioned,

Striving inwardly to penetrate the wild ways of those places,
He searched to see if by chance it might be granted him
To find a living person here also struggling with the zeal
of strong virtue,
One who might bestow the discipline of this service on him.

Given over to these thoughts once in the midst of the heat
Of a scorching day, while he strove to convey
his prayers on high,
He spied a black figure, like a human shape,
racing from the east
And seeking the western slopes, its hair in its hoariness
As white as wool extending down to its neck.
Frightened at this sight, he fortified himself by making
the sign of the cross
On his face, but when he was seen by the one approaching,
He saw it run away with hastening flight
toward solitary places.
He pursued it at a swift pace, trying to catch it.
Now when he began to be near it, with tears welling up
He cried aloud thus, bursting out with these words:
"Alas! Why, Servant of God, do you despise a sluggish,
Decrepit old man by fleeing? Wait, whoever you are,
to be seen.
By Him in whose name you dwell alone in these lands,
Wait! Wait! Turn and be seen. Stay your step,
And by the hope promised as a reward for
such great hardship,
Bless an old man. Stop. Look back. Turn yourself
Toward us, by Him who never rejected anyone."
He repeated such words as he ran, weeping and begging.
They reached a certain place where a riverbed once had
Stood, the dry land burning, the course of
the river vanishing.
Crossing over this place, the body which had fled here
Stood still and spoke these words to the one
weeping and imploring:

'Father Zosimas, forgive me, I pray, since I cannot reveal
Myself by turning toward you; I am a woman
and, behold, in
Place of a bodily covering, as you see, I am naked.
But if you wish to have discourse, throw a garment
to this sinful woman
With which, now covered, she might turn around'.

When his own name was heard, Zosimas was amazed
And, standing in awe, he was filled with great fear.
Realizing that he was known to her
by teaching from above,
He threw his cloak to her at last and turned his face away.
Accepting this, she covered the shameful parts of her flesh;
She turned and begged to know why so great
a father had come.

They lay prostrate on the ground together, and they
prayed to be blessed.
She extended to Zosimas the honor due a priest,
And he offered prayers that God's sublime gifts be
granted to the mother.
Finally, overcome by his many prayers, she spoke thus:
'May You be blessed, O God, caring support of souls'.
Then they arose, and the kindly woman asked the traveler
About the state of the Church, about
the holy monastic order.
He reported that through this pillar of strength
peace was bestowed,
And he entreated strenuously that she pray
for the whole world.
Nor did the mother depart before she
poured forth prayers.
When she began to pray, with her lips moving but
her voice silent,
With eyes and hands raised toward the heights of heaven,
Her whole body was lifted up completely from the ground,

And she seemed to be held up a cubit's length
                    from the earth.
Now a trembling arose in the limbs of Zosimas
                    and a wavering
In his mind, and he feared lest perhaps he
                    was being deluded
By a false spirit, and he lay prostrate, while
                    the woman, conscious
Of this, turned and raised up the monk and drove
                    away his fear.
She showed his error; by her speech she
                    proved her humanity.[1]
Moreover, declaring that she had been washed
                    by holy baptism,
She made the sign of the cross on her forehead,
                    lips, and breast,
And asked the Lord to deliver her from the snares
                    of the enemy.

Again prostrating himself, Zosimas embraced her feet
                    With loud lamenting, pouring forth streams
                    of tears, praying
And asking her to swear by the power of God above,
                    Through Christ Our Lord who deigned to be born
                    of a virgin,
That she not conceal who she was, when, why and whence
                    She came there, and her reason for traversing
                    the vast wilderness.[2]
Declaring, moreover, that he believed he was sent to her
                    for a reason,
Namely, so that the works of God which she had done
                    might be manifest,
Whose judgments it would be unjust to oppose.
Unless it were pleasing to Him that she tell about her life,

---

[1]*Humanam favillam* in the text literally means 'human ashes'.
[2]Literally, *vasta eremi* means 'vast stretches of wilderness'.

He would not have brought her to him to be
seen by chance,
Nor would He have allowed him to endure
such great hardship
And to have made so great a journey, a man who was weak
And broken by the feebleness of old age, as she could see.

Moved by these and other pious words, the woman raised
Him up from the ground and began to speak thus:
'Father, forgive me; it is shameful to weave stories of
Vices and to enumerate for you the squalor of my deeds.
But since you have seen me naked, without a covering,
I shall also lay bare the scandalous sins that I committed.
You will be able to know how very lustful a person I was,
How filthy in my great wickedness and foul in my faults.[3]
Nor indeed does glory shine in my soul, as you think.
How do I refuse in my pride to recount my story to you?
Or what boasting of a polluted woman remains in me,
Who was chosen by the devil, a vessel of perdition?[4]
But I fear lest perchance, when I have begun to lay bare
The infamy of my shame, you will flee me like a snake,
Not allowing yourself to hear what I have basely done
with my body.
But yet I shall tell and not be silent about my
deeds of wickedness.
First, as a suppliant I ask with my most profound prayers
That you not fail to ask pardon for me at the last,
on the Day
Of Judgment, and to benefit me through Christ's pity'.

The old man in his compassion stood drenched
in profuse tears,
And the woman began to tell the story of her life thus:

---

[3]Here I have tried to preserve Flodoard's alliteration: *Quam magni sceleris
squalens et sordida naevo.*

[4]Flodoard's word for 'devil' is *Zabulus* (a corruption of *diabolus*), a name
used by Lactantius in *De mortibus persecutorum* 16.

'I own that Egypt was my homeland and my
parents were Egyptian.
Now, at twelve years old, disdaining their love,
I came in haste to the walls of the city of Alexander.
But it shames me to disclose the squalor and
to discuss the guilt
With which I abandoned my virginity
for wanton debauchery
So that, surrendered to the arms of lust, I lay in filth.
Indeed, the ardent desire for this was once insatiable in me,
And I spent seventeen years and more revelling in these
Mad passions, and I became a prostitute for the rabble.
Some men did not even have gifts for me that
brought my shame;
I was seeking to harm lewd men not for a price, but for free,
So that ensnaring them, I could produce more for myself.
Abundance of riches did not direct me to do this,
For I lived by begging flax or spinning thread,
And I considered seductions to be the highest good.
Thus, while I was defiling my life in such a manner
By shameful acts, I saw at about harvest-time certain men
Of Egypt and Libya proceeding toward the deep sea.
I heard that they were hurrying to adore the relics
of the cross
Whose feast was to be observed soon at Jerusalem,
And, with distaff and spindle cast from my hands,
I ran to them.
I saw that they were strong and suited to practices
pleasing to me.
Approaching the youths who were by chance
spread about on shore
And placing myself in their midst in a coy fashion, I said,
"Take me with you, men, as your friend, for I shall act
In such a way that I cannot seem ungrateful."
They laughed, amused by these and other words.
They took me on the small ship in which they
sailed the deep.

How can I even recall what acts were now shamefully
Done when the sea-voyage had begun? For what tongue
Is able to tell, what ear might bear to catch the
sound of deeds
So black in which I stood forth as the very mistress,
Deeds which I performed on the sea-voyage and
on the land-journey,
Forcing the unwilling and adding incitements
for the willing ones!
Forgive me, Father! I am astonished that the sea
did not swallow
Me, and I marvel that the gaping earth did not
devour me, who,
Worst of women, cast so many men into the
snare of death.
But I think the Lord, who wishes to lose no one
And wills that all be saved, bore this with a patient heart,
Seeking to convert me also, and not ready to condemn me.
Arriving finally at Jerusalem, I supported myself
for some days
Before the feast and performed very vile deeds.
I did not think it enough that youths on the journey were
joined to me:
I added citizens of the place and elsewhere
whom I constrained.

'Thus, when the day came on which the exaltation
of the holy cross
Was observed, I went dallying before a bustling
crowd of youths,
Enticing their souls with debauchery, and I came
before the doors
Of the blessed church. As I tried to enter
the consecrated house,
I was repulsed, driven back by a heavenly strength.
Then I mingled again with the crowds, and again
I was repulsed.

Three and four times I stood striving
with the others entering;
I alone was held back outside by the force of a higher glory.
Now, hardly satisfied that I deserved
to endure this refusal,
I began to ponder within myself in silent accusation that
This happened because of the terrible gravity of my sins.
Thus, while I lamented in sorrow and walked
about the entrance
Beating my breast, I sighed from the depths of my soul.
Full of sadness, I looked upon the doors; I cast my eyes
upon the building.
I saw that a picture bearing the image of Christ's mother
Had been made on the wall through handicraft.
To observe this likeness more closely, I approached in haste
And, gazing at it constantly, I spoke these words
in a whisper:
"Mother of God, I see that I am unworthy to be
part of your
Veneration, defiled as I am by deeds
of such great sinfulness,
You who are beautiful in your venerable soul and
pure in body,
You who bore with undefiled flesh the Lord of the world.
Indeed, I know that my filthy acts are properly
abhorred by you,
But I hear that Christ received his sacred body
from your body
On account of our sins that needed expiation.
I pray, then: Bring aid to one who has solace nowhere now
Save in you and your Son. I beg you, order the sacred doors
To be opened to me; Mistress of Heaven, allow me
to look upon
The royal marks of the sacred cross on which he suffered
with his body.
Take me in your trust, allow me now to be
without the uncleanness

Of lust, and after I see the sacred scepters—
Behold, with the excess
And pomp of the world abandoned—I shall go forth,
Blessed One, to the place where you summon me."

'After these words were spoken, I quickly
approached the doors
As if I had been commanded, inflamed at heart
with the strong fire
Of faith and as if guided by the tenor
of the Virgin's commands.
Coming to the crowds entering, I was joined
to them and went in,
And with no one preventing me, with the way made for me,
I was admitted to the church, I viewed the precious wood
Of the blessed cross, I stood trembling
at the heavenly rites.
I sensed that the compassionate Judge, ready
to forgive all my sins,
Wanted me to open up the heart that grieved me.
And prostrating myself on the stone floor, I
kissed it, and going out
From there to the place where the Virgin's
image was displayed,
I genuflected, confident that I was seeing
her true countenance,
And as a suppliant I added these words of entreaty:
"See, My Lady, you have shown me how great your mercy
Is by accepting the prayers of your unworthy servant.
Your glory was seen by me, which did not warrant
Being seen by us who were crushed by a heavy
weight of vices.
The highest glory be to God, who, through you, receives
All whom true conversion leads to the way of life!
But why should I say more, when now the time is here
For fulfilling promises? O Guide, direct me
where you please,

And show me the way. Lead the way,
O Mistress of salvation."

'When I had said this, I heard a voice
declaring these counsels:
"After the Jordan has been crossed, you will find
a blessed repose."
Believing that the voice was sent to me by God
above, and begging
Our Lady not to forsake me, I left the entrance
of the church.
A certain man, seeing me weeping, gave me three coins.
Having bought loaves with these, I departed straightway.
As soon as I had settled upon the journey
to the Jordan, then
I entered the shrine of John the Baptist; in the evening
I took part
In the sacred rites. Nourished by a meal
of bread, at daybreak
I reached the river Jordan, which I crossed in striving for the
Desert wasteland, looking for the Lord who saves the poor'.

Here Zosimas sought to know the course of her life,
how many years
Had passed from the time when, forsaking the world, she
had come there,
What sustenance she received, what hardship the
hardy woman bore.
She recalled forty-seven winters since she had
come to Jerusalem,
And after that she had dwelt in the wilderness.
She remembered that she had given herself
for daily sustenance
Small pieces of the loaves which she had carried
as she set forth.
'Why do you seek the rest', she said, 'for the rest I fear,
Lest I suffer what I long ago suffered, if I try to disclose it?

Yet, believe me: at that time I endured things as offensive
      As if I lay submersed in a sewer of wantonness.
For indeed, the struggle with worldly desires, which
Empty pleasure, not unknown to me before, used to bring
      Was a very heavy burden for seventeen years.
For indeed, the fishes and flesh of Egypt entered my mind;
      Desiring wine, I was not able to find water.
Sometimes wanton songs returned to my mind,
Songs which I was accustomed to sing charmingly.
Then weeping and vigorously beating my breast,
      I brought back to my heart the words that I
            had formerly spoken
To the face of the Virgin, placing myself before her
            in my mind
And, importunate, I asked that my soul become clean.
During this time a light coming from above surrounded me
      And made me steadfast, meek and strong again
            in my struggle.
But with what words shall I recount the ardor of my lust?
For a strong flame from within burned my flesh,
And desire utterly seized me and exceedingly drew me,
      Driving me toward shameful practices of filthy sin.
Suffering this, and falling to the ground and flooding it
With tears as I saw in my mind the Virgin's countenance
Standing before me, I meditated on the tenor of my faith
      As I lay prostrate looking at the face compelling me
            And frightening me with a menacing
                  expression and pronouncing
Punishments of fury, and showing the wrath of the
                  Judge with His
      Sword of vengeance. Neither did I rise up
                  from the ground
Before that conquering light of heavenly solace that
                  poured over me
      First put to flight the raging passions
                  from my troubled heart.
For I always begged the assistance of the Virgin, Our Lady;

She brought help, and she contended with me,
And even now she herself guides me in all my actions'.

When Zosimas asked then about her food and clothing,
She said that for the years of her great
struggle mentioned earlier
She lived on the two loaves and a half which she had
brought with her,
And after that on plants which she found;
That she was much assailed by the force of the sun,
by the force
Of the cold, when the passage of time took away the
clothes she had.
But, protected in soul and body by the power of God,
She was nourished and clothed by the fortification
of God's word,
Since man does not live only by the solace of bread,
But by every word that comes forth from the mouth
of the Lord,
And those stripped of vices are granted the protection
of the Rock.[5]

When he heard the words of Sacred Scripture,
the noble man
Asked whether the wise woman was
acquainted with writing.
She said no, and taught him that the living word of God
Illuminated her innermost heart and
supplied her understanding.
Then the suppliant begged Zosimas to pray for her,
And imploring him, she asked that he not make
her known publicly
Until she had forsaken the bonds of the flesh, but
that he depart
And visit her again at the same time in the coming year,

---

[5]*Petra*, 'the Rock', clearly refers to the Church. The scriptural reference in the preceding lines is to Dt 8:3. Cf. Mt 4:4; Lk 4:4.

During the time when the holy fasts return
in their usual way;
[She asked] That he not spend the year wandering
again the Jordan
Wilderness, foretelling that he would not be able
to go anywhere
If he tried, but that he remain waiting for the
blessed supper which
Christ's blessing founded; then he should arise
in the evening
And bring to her the mysteries of the Lord's Body,
and sustain her
With the gift of Christ on the bank of the Jordan, where
Coming soon she might partake of the nourishing gifts.
Then she exhorted the Father of the
monastery (designating him
By this name) to be watchful, to guard what had been
entrusted to him,
To attend to his flock, to cut away the improprieties that
he would see.

After these words, he sought out his monastery, she
her remote places.
And so, the Father kept silent for the whole year about
what he had seen,
But when now the holy fasts rapidly approached, he
remained behind,
Assailed by fevers, while the rest were going
outside the walls,
As the old woman had said to him when she prophesied
with her blessed mouth.
But when the brothers returned on the evening
of Holy Thursday,
Zosimas, preparing to attend to her sweet admonitions,
carried with him
In a chalice the sacrament of the divine Body and Blood
to the shore

Of the Jordan, awaiting her arrival on the edge
of the holy bank.
Awaited for a long time, at last arriving
at night-time, she stepped
Across on a bridge prepared for her by the sign
of the cross,
And her solid body walked over the
liquid waves. Observing
These things beneath the moonlight, the old
man was astonished,
And he saw how he was not her equal in the
struggle for perfection.
Then the mother asked that the Creed be recited,[6]
And next that the rich prayer of Christ be added.
After she received the mysteries of everlasting life,
Then she prayed to be dismissed in the peace of God.
But constrained by the man's requests, she ate
Three lentil seeds brought by the old man in a basket.
Then she asked that in the coming year the old man
Return to the stream where they had
talked together before,
Recalling that God ordered her to be seen there.
Thus, begging that mutual consolations be
brought to them,
And that devout prayers be poured forth on both
sides, they departed.
Then, while the blessed old woman again walked across
the water of the stream,
The father, full of joy, sought again the walls
of his monastery.

Returning when a year had passed, he revisited
the designated places,
And on arriving, he saw that now her limbs were forsaken
by their warmth

---

[6] I translate *ordo fidei* as 'the Creed'.

And her corpse, with hands folded, was lying turned
toward the sunset.
The noble man was bathed in tears, and
while reciting prayers
And psalms suited to the occasion, he performed
the funeral rites.
But, not knowing her name, he hesitated.
Looking down at the ground, he saw letters drawn
in the dust
Declaring both the day of her death and her name.
Thus, he concluded that Mary had died during the night
In the place where she had participated in
the sacred mysteries
In the year gone by, and that she had returned in the
space of three hours
To the place which he had barely reached in ten days.

And so the old man was distressed, since
tools and implements
Were lacking with which he might attend to her burial.
Observing a small piece of wood lying by chance
on the ground,
He seized it and, struggling, he pierced the hardness
of the earth,
Wearing out his back and not making progress, unequal
to the toil.
However, drenched in the sweat of his
labor, exhausted, panting,
He looked behind him and saw that a huge
lion stood nearby
And with a gentle tongue it licked the feet
of his dear sister.
Trembling with fear, he fortified himself with the sign
of the cross,
And perceiving at last by its movements that the
lion was fawning,

He thought that this ally was sent to him to carry
out these duties.
He told the faithful beast where to turn over the soil
And to prepare a grave quickly for her blessed limbs.
With its acquired gentleness, the beast obeyed the
old man's orders
And, forgetful of its fury, unacquainted with servitude,
The fierce lion at last learned to serve a holy work;
With a free heart it carried out its servile deeds.
After the funeral duty had been performed
in this different manner,
The different companions returned home,
taking different directions.[7]
The lion, going to the desert, sought the hidden haunts
of wild beasts;
The monk, returning to the monastery, went to the
company of his brothers.
He reported the mighty works of Christ which he
had merited seeing.
The brothers began to celebrate the feast
of the blessed woman,
And Zosimas, an old man of many years, rested in peace.

[7] I have retained Flodoard's play on the word *diversus* in these lines.

HILDEBERT
OF LAVARDIN

THE LIFE OF
SAINT MARY OF EGYPT

THE LIFE OF SAINT MARY OF EGYPT*

CANTO ONE

Just as winter does not nip laurel, nor fire burn gold,
So neither riches nor glory did vex Zosimas as a boy.
Things which quickly perish and those which teach harm
He spurned, renounced, and removed from his
mind and hand.
When he became a monk, he was vigilant in the work
of a monk,
And resolving to follow the teachers of justice and equity,
He insisted upon restraining the law of his own years:
He insisted, and in a short time, with the ways
of his age changed,
He surpassed the ways of his teachers as their teacher.
As his weak age passed beyond the boundaries of boyhood,
His gifts grew, and at the same time his crown increased.
For him nothing was a greater burden than to pamper his
limbs with rest;
Nothing was more unpleasant than not to punish his guilt.
The witness of this was little sleep, rough clothing
And food and bedding; now glory, but then torture.
The witness of this was the monk's color, and flesh
unknowing of Bacchus:
Not flesh, but a thin hide, pale, worn down by whippings,

*The latin text of *Vita Beatae Mariae Aegyptiacae* can be found in volume 71
of the Patrologia Latina, and in a new, recently published edition: *Hildeberti Cenomanensis Episcopi Vita Beate Marie Egiptiace*, ed. Norbert Klaus Larsen. Corpus
Christianorum, Continuatio Mediaevalis 209, Turnhout: Brepols, 2004.
    Although I have not attempted a verse translation, I have preserved the line
by line structure of each canto. Readers of Latin may still delight in the steady
cadences of Hildebert's leonine hexameters, in his classical allusions, in the
word play of his poetry. I hope that the literal translation provided here makes
his distinctive tribute to Saint Mary of Egypt accessible to English readers.

Taught to struggle against itself, taught to serve the spirit.
Amidst these torments, the melody of his holy mind
used to sing
Hymns to Christ whenever his tongue was silent.
His mind, ever conscious of what is right, did
not separate itself
From the corruption of the tomb. God knew this;
man knew otherwise.
In such ways, while he pressed on zealously
with psalms and songs,
He saw the mysteries of Heaven and of things to come.
He saw and he learned, and with such hope
he won many battles.

Captivated by hope, Zosimas increased in holy
deeds just as
A pond grows from a stream or a sluggish fire from olive oil.
And he was mindful that morals are beneficial, mindful
of avoiding applause;
When he fought well, he took care that his fame
did not soar.
The more care he took so much the more did it soar,
And against his wish it reported every
work as praiseworthy.
Countless people came there to be taught, whom he taught
As their position, age and rank demanded,
Excelling the greater ones as the moon excels lesser stars.

While Zosimas accustomed himself to these things,
his pride increased,
And he said these words to himself: 'Whatever right order
and justice bid,
I choose, I follow, I love: I proclaim what must be
learned and retained.
Great hardship and scant sleep weaken my limbs.
These things I chose as a boy, and as a boy I accomplished
these and more.

Now I am the leader of the flock, the oar and anchor
of the law;
Now I am worthy of heaven, holy in deed,
thought and word.
Alone have I fought with the world to a favorable end.
Admiring these things, the people, the clergy, the
flock of monks
Seek me, hear me, love me and do what
my voice proclaims'.

While Zosimas was boasting of such things and
of his merit,
A certain man, to whom the spirit revealed his failings,
disclosed them to him again:
'Now you have struggled well; you have overcome
well where permitted.
Nothing contends with you; your flesh serves,
your mind rules.
But yet the end of this struggle is doubtful, and when you
can be subdued,
You should not say "I have conquered".
For who conquers or is conquered is shown in the end.
The rewards of the victors depend on the end of the toil;
As Scripture says, "the end crowns, not the fight".
When you fight well, when you think all is accomplished,
Pride, which attacks afterward, remains to be conquered.
Unless this is conquered, the promised crown is denied.
O grief! a faithful man is oft overcome by these weapons;
Under this leader a rose is sometimes turned
into a thorny shrub.
Remember, if you will, to stand opposed to that monster,
And do not presume so much to call yourself holy,
Or to say that you are deserving of God's promises
before the saints.
There are many who surpass you on the scale of life;
So that you might know them, ask at the banks
of the Jordan.

There a band of monks worships the King of Heaven.
When you dwell with the monks, do what they do,
avoid the rest.
Hurry, go! delaying means a mighty ruin'.

He went, he departed quickly, and he knocked at the
gates; they opened.
Then, the abbot was greeted, and he spoke these few words:
'Why do you come here? Explain'. Zosimas said, 'I wish
to be instructed,
And I wish that the great heap of my sins
might be disclosed'.
The roughness of his clothing, his suppliant voice, the
grace of his countenance,
And the signs of his holy mind supported
the petitioner's prayer,
And the father responded: 'No one, dearest brother, no one
Cleanses the soul of sickness except the Creator
of the world.
Ask that your bad ways be curbed and, then, that your
good ways be instructed.
Yet, if this assembly pleases you, or this peaceful place,
If, a great palm, you wish to be joined to small shrubs,
You may stay. See if the humble habits of this
sheepfold are beneficial
And choose with us the mallow of this place as your fodder.
The greatest of shepherds will nourish us with his own food,
Food feeding the mind that hungers for nothing after this.
Nothing is more satisfying to the soul than to be fed by
the sight of Him'.

Indeed, Zosimas agreed to these conditions
and remained there.
He remained, and in his new life in his cell,
increasing as much
By the encouragement of the monks as by the
brandishing of weapons,

He saw fierce battles; he praised, learned , served and loved.
It was the concern of this band of monks, the delight of
this excellent band
To hear teachers of the law, to instruct the young,
not to favor
External appearance, to value justice, to keep the laws,
To say nothing rashly, to avoid wrath, envy, strife,
Curses and pride as if they were deadly poisons.
They did not touch salt, fish, wine, pottage, straw or
Linen; they held it a sin to use such things.
For them there was no taste of herbs, no property, no
mention of possessions;
There was no adornment for the hair, no
thought of wealth.
No one envied the abbot because of the cost
of his clothing or
The disparity of his table, nor, in fact,
did brother envy brother.
Their food and clothing were equal, and tumult
was far removed.
Their drink was the river, their festive food
was edible plants,
Their clothing was goats' hair, their hard belts were rope,
Their joys were the return of the fallen, their sorrow the
straying of the fallen.
Their reading the *Lives of the Fathers*, their admonition
the harmony of brothers.
Their conversation was about God or the holy deeds
of pious people.
Because of their watchful ways, leisure was far off, a psalm
was in their mouth,
Their flesh was weakened by much torture and
by rare warmth,
And the flesh made known its works by weeping and
by frequent retreats.
None of these men knew public rumors, the markets,
External affairs or the changes of customs.

The reason for this was their secluded abode,
       their closed doors,
Their stern doorkeeper, a flock and shepherd that
       were both austere.
Those men of the cloister had no established officials nor,
       Except for their shepherd, did they have a prior.
If a matter demanded something or the father
       saw the need,
The concern of each monk was to obey both the matter
       and the abbot.
Indeed, the shepherd showed what had to be done, and
       he did it
Himself, a prelate prepared to be a servant more than
       all the rest.
He was not accustomed to exhort more than to serve.
He was an ornament of the blessed and a mirror for monks.
He was a light in the darkness, cloistered there,
       but everywhere renowned.
He was the primacy of morals, a school of justice, a
       whipping-rod of guilt,
A cross to himself, a model to his flock, a way to Life, a
       glory to the law.
He was known to rejoice for one rejoicing, to grieve
       for one grieving.
Severe to these, mild to those, he became all things
       to all men.

Canto Two

My story reminds me to set forth certain things which the
       monks used to do.
At the time when the people, purified by holy baptism,
       began to pay
Tithes on the sum total of days for the forgiveness of sins,
The monks also went forth from their cells to new battles,
But first each one, having confessed his transgressions
       to the abbot,

Strengthened his soul beforehand and benefitted his body
  With the healing taste of the sacraments and of food.
  Then the customary blessing was sought. It was given,
    They exchanged kisses, and then at last the
            gates were opened.
  After farewells were said, and both the company and
          place were left behind,
  The band of monks went forth at once, separated, and
          entered the desert.
  As custom demanded, some of them remained at home
  Not to guard their goods which were accessible to a thief,
  But lest the cell should be without the holy offices.
  It was made ready by sacred studies and prepared by
  Cleansings of the soul; it was poor in feasting, rich in virtue.
  Having left their house and openly avowed their retreats
          and their spirit,
  The monks went forth, each separately, to whatever place
          his choice took him.
  With equal vows and with witnesses removed,
          each one strove,
  Prostrate, to sing psalms, to wash away guilt with tears,
  To please you, O Christ, with the sufferings of torn flesh,
  To rejoice in you as his companion, leader, end and rest.
  Each alleged you to be his defence in battle, each made
          you his witness,
  Each awaited you as his crown, each had you as his help.
  They pursued their studies and to an equal
          degree they sustained
  Their hearts with holy words, their flesh with roots or herbs.

  Some of them had bread; the fruits of palm trees refreshed
      Some of them instead of tables of delicacies:
  The acorn or the wild olive refreshed them instead
          of the festive banquet.
  Each gathered these things in the desert at a certain time,
    And at certain hours each took rest and a little sleep.

After this regimen had been completed so
for thirty-nine days,
The cell was returned to again; when mass was celebrated,
They returned with palm branches according to the
canon of Christians.

Canto Three

Since Zosimas admired these customs and was prepared
to endure them,
He deemed nothing to be holier than the observance
of this rule.
As soon as the revolving of the season directed him,
he went forth;
He went forth and proceeded from his cell to new battles.
Carrying bread according to his needs, he
crossed the Jordan,
And, thus, having entered the retreats and recesses
of the desert,
He fulfilled his vows to God, he pondered new canticles
in his heart,
He spent his life alone, and his holy deeds proved
him a hermit.
From the time it grew light, he continued his journey;
at night he rested.
Prostrate on the ground, he wept; he sought and prayed
for a companion
Who might assuage his cares and also suffer them,
who might instruct
Him by actions and by overcoming teach him to overcome.
He obtained what he asked for, and a companion for the
way was found,
For when he took longer than usual at the hour
when he sang
The psalms, he saw a certain person as if running,
but without clothing,

And he was greatly frightened, since he thought it
was a phantom.
Agitated by the sight, he recovered through the sign
of the cross.
Then, with his strength put forth, he followed the path
of the one running.
He ran, and neither toil, age nor the haunts of wild
beasts hindered him.
Hurry, Holy Old Man! You are about to see things better
than you hope.
What you see and follow are the footprints of a woman;
A woman goes before you, a woman who is
not inferior to you.
As with her foot, so with her life does this
hermit surpass you.
By her retreats she has so earned merit that now she
is renowned everywhere.
In her retreats she learned well to conquer the world. She
conquered, this woman
Stained by rain-storms, black from the sun, bent by old age,
Hairy in her exposed parts, uncovered in parts that
should be covered.
The scant, snow-white hair on her head grew rough,
Scarcely touching her shoulders, scarcely touching her neck,
Uncombed, straggling, accustomed to diffuse
itself without order.
The woman was whole before, but now her whole flesh
despised that whole;
Now the whole woman was at war with her whole self.[1]
The woman successfully disdained mortal companions,
And with a swift pace she fled from Zosimas who had
been met by chance.
Zosimas followed her and asked her to stop, but she
went on nevertheless.

[1]Here I have retained Hildebert's repetition of *tota* in the Latin.

He cried out more loudly than usual: 'Go more slowly,
whoever you are.
Wait! I am hindered from advancing by fatigue
and old age.
Wait for a weary man. I am not a wild beast.
Hold your step.
I am a small thing, indeed, but a man, a sinner, and I
Acknowledge the same Christ, I visit often the
sanctuaries of monks;
Here I sigh for pardon for my transgressions.
Do not run away. Stay a little while. Fear the haunts
of wild beasts,
For the sake of Christ's name, for the rewards that
you have merited.
Servant of God, stand still. Bless me. Grant what I ask.
Do you not dwell in this wilderness for Christ?
Why do you not listen, at least, because of Christ's name?'

She stopped, and, covered over by her hands, she said:
'Zosimas, I am a woman foremost in acts of sin.
Devoid of clothes, I am embarrassed at the sight of men,
And modesty for my uncovered groin does not allow me
to face you,
But since I know that you are a servant of Christ, what
you seek will happen,
If you give me something by which I might conceal
a woman's shame.
You want me to speak or to stand still; then turn away
and give me clothing'.
Then his cowl was given; the woman was clothed
by it and said:
'Father, why do you pursue the hidden retreats
of a wretched woman?
Why, or where is your course? Here the lion roars,
the bear growls.
What good can you hope for in this land of lions?'

While she spoke these words, the monk was
prostrate before her;
He prayed to be blessed, but the woman, also stretched
out on the ground,
Addressed him as 'Holy Father'. The monk saluted her as
'Most Holy Mother'.
Each cried out 'Bless me', and each pressed the other
for a blessing.
This was the cause of their strife; this was the
hermit's sole strife.
The rest of their life was harmonious and without strife.
While they contended thus, the holy woman
spoke as follows:

CANTO FOUR

'Father, you offend me if you do not
consider things properly.
You truly offend when you, a man, ask of a woman that
This—which a man ought to grant to a woman—be
granted to you.
Allow me to speak the truth: a transgressor of the law
is he considered
Who asks that those things be given which can
rightly be refused.
You, a man, you, indeed a monk, you, likewise a priest,
Are impelled by these three roles to yield to
a woman's prayer.
By custom the hand anointed with holy oil, whose
Office is the grace of this gift, orders you
To bless a sinful woman, not to be blessed'.

The father replied: 'O Holy Mother, it is clear enough.
It is clear, Holy Mother, how great your merits are.
For although I was unknown to you and far removed,
Nor were you told what my way of life was, what
my order was,

You knew all; you were not even silent about my name.
Those facts teach how great you are and how
pleasing to God.
Therefore, as you please Him, as you move Him,
so you please me.
If you ask, He will give. Ask; your way of life
will support your wish.
Their way of life assists the wishes of the blessed.
God heeds this and pays it worthy rewards.
There is no turning from this on account of the
difference of sex,
Nor is a crown given or taken away according to person.
Grace or merit gives to each one the gift sought'.

The woman yielded to these points and to the tears
of the one begging her.
She rose and, with few words spoken first, inquired:
'What peace is there for the holy churches? What
is their status?
With what zeal of kings is the sanction of laws practiced?
With what care do the people preserve human rights?'[2]
He reported that because of her merits
and blessed prayers
The worshippers of Christ were happy and tranquil due
to joyous peace,
And that faith was flourishing. After this he persuaded her
To pray that what now flourished might not
ever grow weak;
That by the antidote of prayers she might
establish and strengthen
A sense of fairness in the rectors of venerable churches.
He said more things besides; she obeyed, prostrated
herself and prayed.
In her soul she rose to heaven, she gave thanks in silence,

---

[2]I have translated *mortalia jura* as 'human rights'.

Her soul entreated in secret without any outcry, and her
Gestures gave signs of an outcry, but her mouth
made no sound.

While she prayed thus, Zosimas was amazed,
and he revered
Her mouth, her hair, her face—all possessing much piety—
And her pale cheeks now full of the foreboding of death.
All the assertions of blessed men are that
Whatever was seen, it bore witness to her virtue.
But things more wondrous than the ones told occurred,
For while she put forth at length the various songs of her
Divinely-inspired heart, she hung as if suspended in the air,
Now entirely removed at a distance from the earth,
And as if she were unwilling to endure contact
with the earth.
Then her purified body remained raised on high.
Thus before the eyes of the monk she was a guest
of those above
For an hour, the woman's flesh to be joined
to those above forever.
At such occurrences Zosimas was sorely afraid and
thought it an
Evil omen or something which was truly dissonant
from the woman.
But she taught him that he was deceived, and she won
back the brother
Who, badly agitated, returned to himself. He was
recovered by these words:
'Ah! where are you carried off to? What are you doing,
Father? Why are you
Troubled? What is this stupor of mind? I perceive well
that you perceive badly.
You have sinned against me when you thought
me a phantom.
I am a woman of wretched fortune, a criminal more
than a woman.

I am mortal flesh, palpable, material and, if you
do not know,
Flesh which lives because of a soul, which
needs food, which
Is changed by time, which warns of blood and ashes.
This which I am now I can give assurance of myself,
But what you have seen, what you were amazed
at while nearly
Speechless, is not attributed to me, for God effects this.
If something virtuous is done, it happens through the
work of Heaven;
If either you act rightly or think rightly, it also
comes from above.
We are a mere shadow, we are smoke driven by a storm,
We are hay of the field, flesh first and filth afterward.
The shape of things perishes, and another is
given every day.
While thus we are changed, we also in silence
bear witness to
What a thing promises to become, where our
nature sends us,
What we are or will be, where we are going and whence
we have come.
All things are certain announcements of humankind's end'.

CANTO FIVE

Afterward, when Zosimas believed that nothing came
from this woman by chance,
He acknowledged his fault and begged forgiveness
with suppliant prayer.
He urged her with tears and with the most profound sighs
Not to conceal anything from him, but that she reveal
what she was, from where,
By what nourishment she was sustained,
who accompanied her.

And the father added these words: 'Answer,
O Most Holy Mother.
It will be useful to be heard; Christ wants these things
to be disclosed.
He suggested this journey to an old man, and with Him
as a guide I came.
He gave me little to fear in the land of wild beasts,
He directed my steps. He fortified a weary man
with his strength.
He mitigated the coldness. He taught me to
endure the heat.
Unless God had aided him, who could have
borne such hardships?
I have come through the haunts of lions
for a particular good.
From there let it be carried back to where it will be
a glory to Christ.
Let this torch, this renowned jewel go forth
from these hidden places.
God does not want the illustrious lights of the world
to be concealed,
By whose rays the winter of souls is relieved.
Therefore, report what you have done, for the
praise of Christ.
How well it is recounted, by this is our neighbor edified!
To be silent about moral lessons is truly a sin'.

He spoke these words and returned to his prayers
with abundant tears;
The woman lifted up the prostrate man and addressed
the one uplifted:
'Woe to me! How many tears am I asked to remember?
What series of wicked deeds and what worldly contagion
Do you seek out, my Father? Do you strive to know more
than my sin?
Whom would I not shock if I should set forth
in order my life,

A base life, a life to be kept secret, a life that
feared no crime?
What hearing can you grant to a woman's lewd acts?
Or what person mindful of morals might tolerate these
memoirs of shame?
What shall I aim for or what shall I do? To display this
wound causes shame,
But if it is concealed, the remedy for the wound is lost.
Eclipsed by this sad decision, the praise of Christ is lost!
When ills are healed, unless thanks are rendered
on this account,
It happens that guilt returns to the ungrateful person.
Lest I offend so, I shall tell of my shameful life and how
God bathed the sores of my soul with his balm.
It is expedient that I be embarrassed for an hour in the
presence of a monk,
That I might not be so before the face of God in the
presence of the saints'.
She said these words and wept; she blushed and feared
to make report.
She looked upward and she looked down; confusion
altered her expression,
Shame constricted her face, there was profuse sweat
on her whole body.
If a part was begun, it scarcely came to the end.
Finally, reproving the sins of the life which had
been asked about,
With her face covered by her poor attire, she spoke thus:

Canto Six

'The country of the Nile brought me forth
from noble stock,
But after I grew up, I destroyed the reputation
of my family.
Then my father on one side and my reprimanding mother
on the other

Often imparted to me in my tender age the precepts
of a strict life.
Gathering the decrees of decency, my mother, as
is the custom,
Taught me to forget the occupation that virtue
does not commend,
And with threats added, she said: "Be like
the Sabine women,
Offer hope to the chaste; be serious in speech,
modest in expression,
And on your young face let the stern matron prevail.
No one has learned too quickly how
to avoid harmful things;
It is right for any age to strive after modesty."
I remember that my supportive parents warned me
of these things,
But the warnings of each parent were tossed to the winds,
And my decency began to be wickedly despised
from my twelfth year.
Thereafter, my bones took on the shameful heat of passion;
Thereafter, when I realized that the union
of a true marriage was
Banished, and that my sluggishness, my shame
had not yet perished,
I endured the loss of my virginity without recompense.
And lest my parents opposing me might delay my wishes,
I left my homeland and went to Alexandria.

'When I reached the place, I was considered to be a
public place for sin.
Nor was that enough, since, when a man was lacking to me,
I roamed about the districts and, solicited by no
one, I solicited,
Disreputable in my attire, roving in eye,
lewd in expression.
With glances given, I was a crime of nature and an enemy.

My gait was feminine, and my speech declared
me a seductress.
They cried out in public (it makes me ashamed to recall
this woman of shame!).
My whole being cried out (Madness is less troublesome!).
Thus forgetful of myself, the guide and
path of destruction,
I spent every one of my days in stories of sin.
I called the day sad on which by chance I was
admonished about virtue,
Which day, as often as I violated it, I treated
as a solemn festival.
Songs that referred to sin and that taught lewdness
I loved, I learned, and I surpassed mimes with my melody.
And when I could excite worn out dancers or older men
To no passion, then disdaining them, I
enticed young ones.
I bought them with any sort of gift,
And among my partners in sin I
distributed individual gifts
Which the needle and spindle might yield for our use
in this life.
Because of these tools the hand
of the pauper approached;
By these tools a house, sustenance, clothing was sought.
By these a sharer of our desires was granted, and a
successor of our guilt.
How much (for I remember) did abundance
of wine please me?
How earnestly desired was food, from which lust is aided?
And when there are these two mighty enemies of our sex
and time of life,
A third foe is added to them: drunkenness.
Because of these plagues, with me and through me
the world was ruined;
Never was it or will it be able to be burdened
by an equal destruction.

Whoever made me go less astray multiplied
his own troubles,
And I preserved for myself the prize of
always acting wickedly.
When I did not know whom I might surpass in sin,
Through manifold sin, after all others, I
even surpassed myself.
For just as I had first dared going astray and then gave in
to raging desire,
Whatever sin I had committed, I justified the worst evils.
And not even my ripe age put limits on my wickedness.
Hateful in the eyes of God for sins of such kind
and such degree,
I spent three times three years and twice times four.
Behold, on a certain day (but how shall I relate this to you?
How wretchedly I fell!), I saw youths on the shore.
I saw them and enticed them. I asked where they
wanted to go.
Smiling, the first one said: "We are going to Jerusalem".
I inquired whether they might accept a companion. The
same one added:
"If you enlist as a sailor, you will go. Our ship stands open
in the air."
Then I said: "In place of a sailor on a ship, I have
prepared pay for you.
If you seek pay, you will possess me in place of pay.
I have nothing except myself, but if it pleases
you, use me.
I have nothing better. Take the enjoyment of this gift.
By this condition I alone shall satisfy all,
If, from all, sustenance comes to me alone."

After these words had been spoken, the young man made
his way in the sand
And, as if the frivolity of my words had been
scorned, he exhorted
The sailors, he called his comrades, he urged, 'Let's sail!'

I bound my hair, I painted my face for sin,
I threw away my spindle, I girded myself for the
experience of sailing.
I proceeded into the vessel; the sea promised prosperity.
The wind was favorable, the youths sailed with the wind
by their skill,
And for a few hours we made use of the watched coast.
Ah me! Where am I sinking? With what speech shall I
tell the rest?
Grant pardon to a wretched woman; shame impels
me to conceal
Those things, and to recall such great
madness brings terror'.
She said these words and wept, and a blush
filled her venerable face.
Zosimas comforted the weeping woman and entreated
her to recount her story.
She obeyed, and at last she answered thus
the one entreating her:

Canto Seven

'My Father, in that ship I multiplied my sins.
I did nothing there save what was contrary to the law,
And every thought of justice was far from my concerns.
Thus, I wickedly reproached the sailors and directed them
to wicked acts.
I incited the sluggish and I summoned those who
lingered in fear of shame.
The one who found sin pleasing, I considered brave; I
swore that he was blessed.
Taught to serve a man's desire with my whole body,
Through the thousand perils of the sea, my care
was for sin:
To cling to wickedness, to fear nothing except virtue,
To be turned toward passion, to be very often
dissipated by wine,

To be filled with food, to vary the melodies of my singing,
To practice all these things which are hostile to salvation.
Believe me, I marvel much that such sin was unavenged,
That neither sea nor wind destroyed the villainy
of the wicked.
I marvel that the ship served perverse people
for these shameful acts,
That God's wrath did not hinder so many sins,
such great sins,
That the shore and the south wind and the waves
bore this lewdness,
That evils were safe amid almost a thousand
forms of death.
But the Lord Jesus, though offended, knew how to spare;
Though offended, he spared, and in sparing he showed
how to return.
At length the Fount of Mercy freely showed me that,
Although angry, he defers to punish our guilt, and
he is reluctant
To strike, since he seeks to spare our faults'.

Canto Eight

'So that you will not be burdened by the long account
of my passions:
I was brought to port, and, a harlot, I entered
the new city.
Joined to a fickle crowd, I remained in the city as a
foreigner and a foe.
I went around the streets, and I sought
after unjust embraces.
So the citizen, just as the stranger, was
urged toward misdeeds.
While I enticed these men, while I in my raving
joined myself to
Such great vileness, the exaltation of the holy
cross, which was

There at that time, summoned the citizens
to the sacred places.
A multitude of fathers went before, the devotion
of mothers followed.
The almost-empty city compelled me to go, to see, to seek
What was drawing the people, what was pleasing
in the sanctuary.
I went seeking a deadly companion for myself,
and, it shames
Me to say, one who might have intercourse
with a wicked woman.
But later this desire disappeared, and
the mercy from above
Restrained the passions and surges of my incitements.
In fact, wanting to enter the gates and see the holy relics,
I was not allowed to enter them nor to see them.
The open door was receiving the people who came,
But a heavenly force rejected me, a sinner.
While I supposed that these things happened because
of my feminine weakness,
I struggled with as much impudence as I could to go in.
But not even then could I enter through the open doors,
Although people going before and people
following were entering.
I was amazed and angry that I was held back
from the holy sanctuary.
I even mingled with the crowds so that, pushed forward
by them, it might help.
I struggled, and I pushed the people pressing together,
But none of these attempts profited me in my
wish to enter.
My guilt wore out these efforts and weakened them,
And my sin did not allow me to reach the holy entrance.

As I realized this, I spoke thus: 'It was not right that
Those sacred places lie open to me, a wretched woman,

Sacred places to be respected for the glory
of their blessed works.
Here the lamentable covenant of death was broken.
By these works the Creator expiated our deeds; he
became a victim.
Here he was condemned, here he died, here
he was buried,
From here he rose again and brought back life from death.
Having dared to come to places
of such wondrous sweetness,
I did not bring olive oil, I did not bring the
perfume of incense,
Nor a pure soul that would be more pleasing than
all of these.
The stench that bears witness to shameful acts was
readied in place of incense,
And in place of the glory of good morals I bore a
host of disgraces
And whatever wretchedness falls to this kind of women.
Alas! What have I attempted? What kind of woman am
I? Where and whence
Have I gone? A harlot from a vile brothel, I have come to
the table of Christ.
Burdened by these evils, I have come, such a one,
to such places.
Often attempted in vain, this entrance has impeded me.
God hates the shameful acts of the whorehouse and keeps
them from His altars,
And he keeps uncleanness of soul from
his lifegiving nourishments'.
Then I was silent, and I did not withdraw far from there,
But standing before the doors, I was immersed
in welling tears,
And thrice repulsed, I lamented, and sorrow burdened
my groaning mouth.
My emotions were divided, confusion assailed my heart,

And it began to be mindful of morals, to be
ashamed of evils,
And although it was late, although I was buried, I sought
to rise again.
What I rightly sought was granted, and Lazarus came
forth from the tomb'.

CANTO NINE

By chance there was nearby a beautiful picture of a woman
Painted beneath the name of that exceptional Mary
Who bore the Saviour, like a star in its splendor'.
While I gazed upon this, I was changed within, and I
became a different person.
Weeping, I came nearer, I humbled myself before the face
of this woman,
And on bended knee I importuned the mother of our
Father with this prayer:
"To you, pious Virgin, holy Virgin, Virgin Mary,
Virgin of a new rank, I come, but I am a woman of death,
But I am wickedly common, unclean, a woman
of the brothel,
One who has lamented except when I have done things
that should be lamented.
When I committed shameful acts, as if praised
for shameful acts,
I laughed, and many a sad face became cheerful with me
as a concubine.
Every night was entirely sleepless when a man approached,
And I considered it a sin if I did not cover myself
with much sin,
Rejoicing in forbidden intercourse, and
with married people.
So did I fill up the course of my wretched life;
So did I proceed. Now I condemn what I did wickedly,
I repent of going astray, and the foulness of my
frenzy seems sordid.

I shall not suffer, though I am rightly condemned, or I
will love my guilt
If the bolt is loosed by which a sinful woman is detained,
If a wretched woman is permitted to see the Cross of Life.
I hope for this through you; through you I seek to ascend.
For although he is angry, may your Son grant this
with you as suppliant.
Indeed, let him grant this, since he is Father and Son
at the same time.
A double disposition influences his exorable heart;
To any gift you seek, each—Father and Son—is
turned as One.
Therefore, under this covenant, grant to me what I
rightly strive for;
Be the witness of this covenant, and be also the avenger
of my weakness.
I do not want my crime spared if it is repeated."
With these words spoken and vices now relinquished
from my mind, I arose.
I turned away from there, good hope accompanied me
to the sanctuary,
And, impatient of delay, I entered, but without a struggle.
I rejoiced to be admitted, I begged that my
sins be remitted,
I cried out for forgiveness, I bowed before the
banners of salvation.
The sins of my soul frightened me away
from the sacraments;
When these had been exposed, I sought again the
Mother of mercy,
And I gave thanks to one so well-deserving, I
duly prayed that
What she bid would happen, I asked to be taught
where to go.
I sought the way of good morals, I implored their mother
to guide me.
While I pounded so anxiously at the doors of life,

She answered thus (I knew not who was speaking,
I only know that someone spoke in this manner):
"If you cross the Jordan, you will find rest."

Then a stupor came over me which ceased after a time;
Thus admonished, I went forth quickly.
I sought and took the way where one
approaches the Jordan.
While I was hurrying along, a certain man conveniently,
According to the circumstance, offered me three silver
coins and gave
Them secretly. Then I bought three loaves and,
having gone beyond
The city walls, I pressed forward and was carried
forth and withdrew
As an exile from the multitude. It was evening, and
I drew near
The sanctuary of John the Baptist which the
forementioned river flows past
On its gentle course. There, after I professed my
guilt amid tears
And groans, I approached the eucharist
with a contrite heart.
From there I crossed the forenamed river with the bread
I had received;
I sought a way of life by which I might condemn
my former sins.
Then I deprived myself of pleasures of the flesh and
lust of the flesh;
Then I redeemed my time of wickedness
with a better purpose.
But perhaps my words weary you, and the sun that
Cannot be held back hastens along in his swift car.
Therefore, Father, desist'. Then he said:
'Most pious Mother,
Come, tell what followed; nothing is more
rightly made known.

Speak, O Handmaiden of God. A great part of the day
remains and nothing
Complies more with my wishes than that you tell
your whole story.
Come, if you remember, tell what hardships
you suffered there,
Where your food came from, what and where your
clothing came from;
If any temptation waged war with you again and did
not overcome you;
If your former troublesome passion of the
flesh ceased seething'.
Here, moved by the old man's requests, she sat down
on the sand
And, shedding tears, she added the following
to her first discourse:
'My Father, after the failing of my lamentable life,
I completed forty-seven years, and yet I did
not wash away
My sins without a hard struggle, for again
I was tempted, and after my holy vows there was
A return to cups of spiced-wine and excess of foods.
The fishes of Egypt and the desire for wine (which
had been forsaken)
Affected me in my wretchedness and tormented me so
much more violently
The more I turned my attention to banquets and the
zeal for drinking.
While moderation seemed vile to me and
drunkenness was pleasing,
In cities and abroad my vice was
abandoned with difficulty.
Everywhere, in all places, the Enemy assailed my plan
of good morals.
His evil mention of pleasures beset my
insufficiently-strong spirit
And attacked it; Eve raged and troubled the Man.

Eve desired the food of death in the gardens of life.
Ah, me! It shames me to tell certain things, yet I
shall tell them.
Learn that nothing is secure unless it has first been
freed from flesh.
That which threatens and thwarts virtue will
always be present.
I was inflamed with the ardor of sexual union
and the desire
To sing melodies and songs of accursed loves, and
to my mind
That was wickedly relapsing, forbidden embraces
And a thousand married men returned, kisses were sought,
And my wishes wandered toward sexual union.
Virtue was a burden; to be considered beyond the law
caused me no shame.
I loathed the law, I put serious matters after trifles,
A life of wandering alone after crowds, the desert
after city gatherings.
These fantasies assailed my weakened virtue,
And a form of madness stifled the growth of morals in me
Until, turned in prayer to that excellent Mary,
I withdrew my sight from those temptations of my soul.

Thus, I came here, I groaned, I wept, I became a sacrifice,
I sought to be reformed, I prayed for my better ways of
old to be renewed.
After holocausts of prayers my right mind
returned and persisted;
After the weeping of my heart, every thought of
filth fled away.
Through these remedies the abundant temptations
of my mind subsided,
And the medley of renewed shameful acts abated.
That which burned wickedly grew accustomed
to be utterly cold.
Moreover, as I was weeping and wretchedly cast down,

A brightness shone around me and covered me entirely.
It was sent to recall one going astray, to raise
up one falling,
To bring good hope, to bestow strength, to point
out a crown.
Thus, seventeen years elapsed; harsh times
Were mixed with gentle ones, and savage times with mild.
But when I truly wept, the Virgin Mother wiped
off my new wounds
And washed them. Then there was salvation; then I
was at peace.
Through so many years, my food was just the two loaves
That I carried here with me at the time I departed
from the city.
They had become dry and hard, and they had lost
their proper color,
And they had ceased to confer strength, yet
from this source
I was accustomed to relieve my hunger sparingly.
I scarcely found anything that I might drink when
I was weak.
After the loaves had been consumed for a long time,
My mind, clinging to the Lord, withdrew from vain cares.
From then until now my old temptation has subsided.
From then until now my emotion has obeyed reason.
Until now my outer food has been plants with foliage;
Until now my inner food has been the words of heaven.
The clothes that I had, age tore and wore away;
Then, naked, I remained in regions scorched by the sun
Where, enduring excessive cold in the hours of the night
And excessive heat in the hours of the day, I prayed
For the sins and the losses of my past life.
I exchanged hymns for jests, I purged loud
laughter by sorrow,
Punishment atoned for pleasure, thirst for drunkenness,
Poverty for luxury, toil for leisure, juice for honeyed-wine,
Torture for a soft couch, holy devotion for guilt.

I bore just as many torments as I had done shameful acts
in the past.
Whatever sin the flesh had committed, the sacrifice
of flesh cleansed.
What punishments, what sort of struggle
with these punishments,
Or what tortures were renewed equally for me
night and day
God knows, the Witness and the Reward of these labors.
Often under the constellation of the fiery Crab and
in the frozen winter
I grew stiff with the cold of night, I was burned by the
heat of day,
And, secure nowhere, I lay down as if dead.
To this pain was added dust storms and the sand's heat,
Neither was the burden of these lightened by the
conditions of the region,
For the place, as you see, is empty of trees, mountains,
caves and places
By which the heat of the Dogstar[3] is kept away or winter's
cold is warded off.
You know that Mankind does not live soundly
by bread alone,
Nor does a person withstand the winds by clothes
or buildings alone:
God is sustenance for all; God is a whole garment for all.
The King of Heaven rules heaven, and he
sustains the faithful.
When the wind rages outside, the ardor of His love
suppresses the wind;
Neither because of snow nor wind does the soul's
devotion grow cold.
Hope in the starry region is not at all difficult
for good people.

---

[3]The Dogstar, or Sirius, located in the constellation Canis major, is the
brightest star in the sky.

As I had promised myself the world, wickedly partaking
of the world,
No writings for the heart, no reading was a concern
to me, nor anything
Of doctrines or of the soul, only of accursed things.
There had been only one devotion, the sins of lovers,
And to gratify people wickedly in a house of ill repute.
If I undertook again anything of virtue, of morals, of piety,
If I picked up again the counsels of divine books, behold:
It was given by heaven. God taught these, God carried
them into effect.
The Spirit filled my soul without delay and
instructed my words:
There was no toil for me in learning, no
toil in instructing.
Thus have the seasons of my past life flowed by.
The seasons that remain offer me the hope of a reward,
A solemn reward, because the reward is everlasting life'.

Canto Ten

'I have explained in order what I did wickedly or well,
And it did not shame me to disclose what
I shamefully pursued.
There is no reason why you should stay here longer.
The shadows increase, the evening star comes,
the constellations shine,
Night in its customary course orders your return.
Therefore, turn back.
Do not publish abroad what I have entrusted
to you alone.
When your monks go forth from the monastery
And likewise cross the river Jordan,
You will remain, resting at home because of an illness
Which, however, you will get over with the Lord's help.
When you have been made sound, go
forth without delaying,

And remember to bring with you the food of the altar,
Which I hope for in heaven and seek to take
first on earth.
I hope for this pure essence; I seek the essence and the
form of the essence.
Animated by this food I shall go securely where I
strive to go.
For me this is a guide, a bearer, a way, a homeland, a reward.
With this guide, My Father, pursue your way; I
shall meet you.
A certain day will bring you again before these eyes; it
will bring you,
And I shall announce certain things that will
benefit your brothers.
Then, then at last I shall see you for the final time'.

With her farewell said and Zosimas left behind, she
fled from there.
As she departed, not even looking back at his entreaty,
He followed her with his eyes; after he saw her thus
Carried away in swift flight and recalled in vain,
He reversed his steps, turned back and departed.
His cell lay open to him on his return. The woman stayed
fixed in his mind,
The woman remained in his heart, and hardly was she
thought of as a woman.
Thus the appearance of the woman was equal to the
saints on high.
Thus her manner, her face, her humility, her mortal ashes
were not those of a human.
These and almost these alone did he contemplate and
long to see.
These Zosimas sighed for night and day alike.

A set time was selected in which the holy flock
might go forth.

Behold, the set time arrived; the community departed
from its house,
But Zosimas was stricken by illness and compelled
to stay there.
He gave thanks cheerfully because
what the woman-prophet
Had told him was fulfilled. He lay sick, but in due time
he would follow.
Whoever hopes for lofty rewards
willingly endures hardships.
Hope aided the ailing monk, hope cheered him as he lay
in his bed,
Hope pushed back his groaning and his tears,
Curbed his anxieties, relieved his cares,
brightened his face.
He was not deceived by hope, for his former
health was restored;
He was well again in a short time, and the weakness
of his frail age
Did not hold him back. He went forth, and the toil he
longed for was begun.
And as if the woman might be cheered by foods
or various provisions,
He carried with him a pan of boiled lentils,
Adding also the carefully-protected Food of Life.
He undertook his journey during the evening
of the sacred supper,[4]
And, moved by hope and faith, he hastened to reach
the river bank.
As soon as he stopped, sighing he spoke such
words as these:
'Ah, me! in vain have I sought and traveled
about this wilderness:
Either the woman lies in hiding forgetful of an old man,
or she is hindered

[4]Holy [Maundy] Thursday.

By the sands, or she came earlier but departed,
disappointed in her hope,
And while I delayed, she went to the regions
where she dwells.
Perhaps she will come, but what opportunity will there
be for me
Of delivering the sacrament or of speaking
with the woman?
The Jordan stands in the way; to advance on foot is
a useless effort.
In fact, nowhere is there a shallow place nor a bridge nor
a boat anywhere'.

Lamenting much, the sorrowful old man cast
his eyes about;
He gazed attentively into the distance, for his mind and
mouth were still.
Behold, with swift steps, on bare feet, late in the
evening, the woman
Came as she promised, and she visited the old man again,
And barely standing, as if worn out by the hardship
of her journey,
She raised her soul and her serene face
toward the heavens
And, weeping, made the sign of the fruitful cross
on the water.
Thus by this token she crossed the distance of the waters
Between them like one with feet covered with dust.
The world obeys no one who entrusts himself to the world;
The elements know how to favor a pure soul.
Whoever rejoices in good deeds dares to ask for any good
things at all.
One who offers himself without the wound of sin longs
for nothing in vain.
The moon was shining brightly and did not allow her
actions to lie hidden;

By the moon's rays these sights were exposed, and
            from the old man
They wrested and elicited various songs of praise.
Behold, after the darkness was removed, the woman
            and the man
Devoted themselves to pious vows. With holy
            prayer they appeased
The Divinity, they drenched their faces with weeping,
            they interrupted
Their speech with sobs, they prayed
            for sinners, they imbued
Their speech with examples, they rejoiced sincerely, the
            woman in the old man,
The man in the woman. The sum of their speech was
            God or moral lessons.
After these were finished, she approached the chalice
            of God's mercy,
And, having confessed before she would touch any
            part of it,
She offered herself with tears and made herself fit
            for the chalice.
Then, as she knelt, the wedding feast of Life was
            given to her,
And in that drink she was united to Christ,
            her Leader, relating
In such speech to her companion what had been
            entrusted to her:

CANTO ELEVEN

'My Father, examine your brothers'
            transgressions and regressions.
Some of them disdain the teaching of morals and—as if
            they do not know
By what deception the Enemy strives to deceive or
            by what means

He assails the door to the soul—they
disregard the Enemy.
By subtle cunning the wolf lies in wait at the sheepfold.
If the sheep strays anywhere, she dies, stricken
by a wound,
And while she looks back, she is exposed to his bite.
May the care of Abbot John oppose these injuries,
And may he encourage his flock not to spurn
the monk's rule.
To the brother who goes astray, let the rule equal a father
who is not silent,
Since those whom equal guilt binds together, equal
punishment also torments.
Thus did Eli fall when he made sad the King of Heaven.
Lest such a transgression of the rule be his,
may the father
Root out harmful things by virtue of his watchful care.
May he keep watch before the gates, strengthen those
wishing good morals,
Inspire beginners, restrain those who
display immoderate behavior.
May he reprove and encourage them; may he practise
what he preaches.
Stern, may he soothe; gentle, may he make
rough ways known.
May he personally mortify them, may he add scourges
to words in moderation,
May he wash the sores of guilt, or let their
author cleanse them.
Although a man might be secure and happy
following wicked ways,
God imposes a heavier judgment on his bold deeds,
And His great forbearance continues the prosperity
of the wicked.
One who is now tormented does not know how much
he is being purified.
When He rages and strikes us now, God seeks
to spare hereafter.

You will relate these words and return here yet once more;
Go! See your flock again, order them to respect the rule,
And while you stand at the altar, pray
for this sinful woman'.

After she spoke so, she went back, and the waves yielded
to her as she went;
She walked above them with dry feet, proving that she
was a servant of God,
And, while Zosimas stood there
in amazement, she vanished.
He went home in haste; and, far away from the
woman, he was
Her companion in sincere prayers, and he was mindful
of the woman.
This woman haunted his mind; she alone possessed him
entirely as he
Complained because the year was so long and because it
passed so slowly.
Finally, the year elapsed; the father went forth
and sought her.
When he had gone beyond the gates, he bore
hardships without toil.
With every effort possible, he traveled the roads
on foot, he searched
Other places with his eyes, and, weeping, he prayed
these words and more:
'O Christ, form of the Father, Father and only offspring
of the Mother,
Hear me as I weep; guide me, I pray, as I
follow desolate tracts.
Show to an old man this woman on whose account I have
come with You as guide,
The woman whom I wish for, whom I seek, in whose
heavenly prayer I hope.
Although she now serves in earthly camps, she
inhabits the heavens,

And now as companion of the saints above she scorns
the fleeting nature
Of things; now united to God she seeks this fruit
from her wedding:
Long-lived fruit, the fruit which endures for all time.
Woe to me, woe to a wretched man; through trackless
places in vain
I seek one for whom a populous home is in hiding places
with one inhabitant;
For whom a house is the desert, bedchambers are
an open cave;
For whom modesty is a veil, a companion is an angel,
halls are the open sky.
Where shall I go or what shall I do? Shall I
follow the tract
Scorched by the sun? Many torments—old age,
thirst, heat, sands—
Are opposed to these undertakings, and my
wishes are hindered'.

Having complained so, sorrowful Zosimas cast
his eyes about;
He did not know whether to hurry, and, unsure what way
to choose, he stood fast.
He cried out, he listened, but no voice, no echo
resounded;
No sound was heard, no trace of feet was
found, and while
He wandered about, while he doubted everything in sight,
A ray from above led forth his cold and listless limbs
As if it were his guide and his leader.
Rejoicing in this sign and worshipping the
Lord God, he ran
To that place. He found her whom he sought with prayers
and on foot,
But she was already dead, already joined in fact
to Christ, already

In the castles above, already glowing more brightly
than the stars.
Her flesh to be glorified, purer than melted gold,
Lay covered as was proper for a woman.
How sad was the monk's grief! What was his
anxiety of heart?
What were the groans of his torn soul? What
were his words?
At one moment he sighed, at another he
looked all around;
Now he fixed his eyes on the heavens and did
not utter complaints.
Prostrate, he mourned and respectfully clung to her heels.
He wept over them and apportioned faithful kisses
to those holy feet.
With vows and voice he asked that he not turn back,
Considering it a great gift to attend her corpse
with his corpse,
And with the same death to live and be buried together.

While he grieved and wavered in doubt about her name,
A name found in the sand lifted up the
old man's countenance,
And the gloom of his mind vanished at these instructions:
'Holy Father, I ask that the bones of Mary the
Egyptian be interred;
Let her be buried in the soil, let her ashes be
added to ashes.
As soon as you gave the Body of Christ and His
chalice to her,
The first light of the second day freed the woman
victorious over the world.
After the evening had been spent with the mysteries
of Holy Thursday,
Heavy darkness crept in since the light receded
with the sun'.
By these words doubtful Zosimas finally recognized

Her name and her last day. Who was the author
of this writing?
For he knew that the woman had read nothing, had learned
Nothing of these studies, nor was she even
mindful of them.
From this source he also ascertained that,
when the sacraments
Had been delivered, Mary had been transported here
in a moment
And then had died where he had arrived, weary after a
thirty days' journey,
And had declared that he was overcome by toil.
By weeping he showed the new wounds of his heart.
He sat by the lifeless woman, and the tears of his
abundant sorrow
Overflowed; angry at death, he applied himself
to the duty of mercy.
He sang her praises, he covered her limbs, he
closed her eyes.
Now he embraced the soles of her feet, now he did
homage to her head,
Her hair, her face. Her care for these had been lack of care.
Their splendor was scorn, squalor and want.
The woman was clean enough from tears
summoned by piety;
She was washed by grace since she was a companion to
the saints in glory.

He attended to her burial, devoted himself to this; these
were his concerns,
But he did not know what to do: the hard ground was rigid.
Many things weakened the old man; toil and heat and
thirst tormented him.
His strength yielded to his years, his arms
to winding sheets;
There was no mattock at hand, nor any hoe.

While he was grieving and groaning, a new event took
        his breath away:
His eyes became dry, because better things were
        readied through hope,
For a lion, like one mourning and honoring
        the dead body,
Promising submissiveness and setting aside
        his fierce wrath,
Came with his neck bowed, and with his
        proud ferocity set aside,
The humble beast began to lick her holy feet.
The old man marveled at such a comrade and
        one so devoted.
He attributed it to the woman's merits that the wild
        beast was gentle,
That the lion was mild, that her name adhered to the sands,
That a light had shone above and, going before,
        had led him,
That no wild animal had disturbed her though
        she was unguarded,
Nor had a bird torn her flesh though she was unburied,
Neither had the great, raging heat nor the entire
        year dissolved her.
Now he imagined what glory remained
        through their incorruptibility
For the limbs of the one lying there under the hot winds.
Likewise tried by so many and such great
        hardships, he recalled
All God's gifts; he went over what he might say
While he passed on commands to his comrade
        in such words:
'My companion, we are urged and admonished
        to bury this woman
Whom the world knows not, for whom it was greater to
        be inferior in the world.
But if you have come, sent in Christ's name, if you will be
A servant, dig a grave, and, afterward, go back.

Cast off your frightfulness and forget
your accustomed fury.
What you shall do for this woman becomes
praise of Christ'.
With these words not yet finished, and with his ferocity
and threats abandoned,
The lion came gently forward and was ready to obey him,
And without delay, in the brief space of a fleeting hour,
He fulfilled the command, completing the hurried task.

Meanwhile, the monk lay prostrate before her holy limbs.
No garment covered him except a worn, old cowl
Which, now weather-beaten, scarcely clung to him.
With these coverings he wrapped the limbs of the
one lying there,
Namely the great treasure, the one
already bearing something
Of the splendor, something of the solemn fragrance,
Something excellent from the nectar of the gods.
The woman blessed by the reward of her holy labors
Was carried to the grave and buried with the
wild beast's help.
Then the old man turned back; he ordered the
lion, his servant,
To depart. At home he told what he had seen; he abhorred
Sparing sins. He reproved, he encouraged:
he promised blessings,
He threatened hardships. So, when he had lived one
hundred years, he died.

ANONYMOUS
SPANISH POET

THE LIFE OF
SAINT MARY THE EGYPTIAN

THE LIFE OF SAINT MARY THE EGYPTIAN

[I. INTRODUCTION][1]

Listen, disciples, to a story
Which contains nothing but the truth.
Listen with your heart,
If you would have God's mercy.
Everything is truthfully done
Without a hint of falsehood.
All those who would love God
Will listen to these words.
To those who give no thought to God
This account will be hard to hear,
While it will be heard with ready heart
By those who would love God.
These who would love God,
Will receive great benefit from it.
If you listen to this story
It will do you more good than any fable.

[II. ARGUMENT: GOD'S MERCY]

About a lady of whom you've heard
I wish to tell you her whole life:
Of Saint Mary of Egypt,
Who was a lady of great beauty,
And of her beautiful body,
When she was a girl, a child.

---

[1]This translation is based on Alvar's critical edition, *Vida*, 2:47-107. The subtitles have been added to provide points of reference. They modify those in Alvar's edition.

Our Lord gave her beauty,
Although she was a comely sinner.
The mercy of the Creator
Later bore her great love.
Let every sinner know this,
Who may be guilty before God,
That there is no sin
So great or so horrible
That God will not pardon
Through penitence and confession.
To anyone who repents from the heart,
God gives pardon.
Those who accept penance
Rightly guard themselves from unbelief
Because those who do not believe the Creator
Cannot have his love.

[III. THE NECESSITY OF PENITENCE]

Sin is not a created being
But a disturbance arising in nature.
The God of heaven did not create sin
Although it resides in all people.
In all people dwells
Our wicked sin.
Having found lodging in all people
It incites them to do all evil deeds.
For there is no one born,
However wise he may be,
No one who can be so wise
That he does not sin.
The apostles who served God
Sinned much and failed much;
So there should be no astonishment
That someone may end up sinning;
No more than there is great wonder about someone
Who always sleeps and never wakes up.

Someone who is so fast asleep in his sins
Does not wake up before death.
When such a sinner feels he is dying,
At that moment he repents.
Since everyone dies
One can repent too late.
According to a saying of Saint Augustine,
Such an end is not good,
For once death comes
No one can do evil or good.
When death arrives
No one can do right or wrong.
One abandons evil
When one has no power to do it.
If such a one's life lasted longer,
He would do still more evil.
But when the miserable soul goes there,
Who will any longer save her?
There is no one who saves her,
But God, if it pleases Him.
We all know what will happen,
That each will receive what he deserves.

[IV. MARY UNTIL THE AGE OF TWELVE]

I wish to tell you about a woman
Whose name was Mary.
The name ascribed to her
Indicates that she was born in Egypt.
She was baptized as an infant,
Then she was educated.
While she was a youth
She abandoned goodness and embraced folly.[2]

---

[2]References to wisdom and folly and to two ways are reminiscent of wisdom teaching, such as that in the biblical book of Proverbs.

She was so full of sensuality
That she had no other interest.
Since she was so beautiful and affectionate
She put great faith in her youthfulness.
She so loved to follow her fancies
That she gave no thought to other things
Beyond spending and having a good time,
For she was not mindful of death.
She gave herself to her relatives,[3]
She degraded herself with all men.
I firmly believe that at the time
No other woman lived so wantonly.
No woman but Mary
Was so full of lewdness.
When her parents saw her
It was almost the death of them.
She did not value their advice
Any more than a gust of wind.
'Dear daughter', said her mother,
'Why do you not believe your father?
If you continue your activity
We will have great grief from it.
In God's name I beg you, daughter Mary,
Turn to the right path.
When you have left your current path
We will give you a good husband.
It is not right that you be lost
For lack of material goods in our life.
Daughter, you are of great lineage.
Why are you in misfortune?
You should have honor
Like others of lesser birth.
Your father has withdrawn his love.

[3]The word translated as 'relatives' is *parientes*. Alvar suggests 'friends'. There may be an implication of incest to indicate the degree of Mary's moral corruption.

He will not be satisfied in his lifetime.
He curses the hour when you were born
Because you did not take his advice'.
Thus her mother admonished her
With tears in her eyes.
Mary set little store by it;
She was guided by youthful folly.
From the time she was twelve years old
She did what she desired with all men.
She didn't want to deny herself to anyone
Who had something to give.
Afterward it occurred to her
That she had abandoned her family.
In order better to do what she wanted
She sought to leave their town.

[V. MARY IN ALEXANDRIA]

Mary went into another kingdom
In order to get a higher price.
She abandoned all her kin,
So that she never saw them again.
All alone she left like a thief
Who wanted no companion.
Thus Mary set out on her road,
She who was not looking for company.
She had a bird in her hand;
It sang winter and summer.
Mary held it in high esteem
For each day it sang of love.
Mary went to Alexandria,
Where she sought lodging.
She went there to find accommodation
With the wicked women on the street.
When the prostitutes saw her
They were well disposed to receive her.
They received her with great honor

Because of the beauty they beheld in her.
She caused the sons of the inhabitants to call,
They came to admire her.
They had great pleasure from her
For she was like a flower.
They all went there to court her
And to praise her body.
She received them with pleasure
Because they gave her delight.
And by doing all their sinful pleasure,
She kept them in great content.
In drinking and eating and lewdness
She passed day and night.
When she rose from eating
She went to have sport with them.
So much did she want to play and laugh
That she forgot she had to die.
The young men of the city
She so delighted with her beauty
That each day they came to see her
From whom they could not keep away.
So many companions came there
That the games turned to hard feelings.
At the gates, in the doorways,
There were great sword fights;
The blood which flowed from them
Ran down the middle of the street.
When she saw the sad situation
No compassion gripped her.
Whoever was the most crafty
He was her friend.
She welcomed inside the one who conquered;
She grieved little for the one who died.
If two friends died,
She had fifty who lived.
For the soul of one who died
She would give no more than a laugh.

Those who were hurt because of her
Never received a visit from her.
She preferred playing with the healthy
To visiting the sick.
Mary was in Alexandria;
There she corrupted herself night and day.
She had come to Alexandria;
This was the life she led there.
The moment she entered there
The whole town was stirred up.
So much blood was spilled
That the whole town was diminished.
All the towns around there
Were all in great terror.

[VI. PORTRAIT OF A BEAUTIFUL SINNER]

Of the beauty of her appearance
As it is described in writing—
Before going further
I would say something of her appearance.
From her time on
No one else so beautiful was born;
Neither queen nor countess,
No other has been seen like her.
She had round ears,
White as ewe's milk.
Black eyes and eyebrows,
A brow white to the hairline.
Her face was tinted with color
Like a rose in flower;
Her mouth beautiful and well-proportioned.
Her gaze was very beautiful.
Her neck and her breast
Were like the flower of the thornbush.
Her breasts showed healthy development;
They were like apples.

Her arms, her body, all of her
Was white as crystal.
Her figure was well-proportioned;
She was neither fat nor very thin.
She was not tall or short,
but just the right height.
We have to leave her beauty now—
It is not possible to portray it to you—
To say something of her clothes
And of her adornments:
The worse day of the week
She did not wear clothing of wool.
It took much silver and gold
For her to dress according to her desire.
She wore expensive gowns
Over which she wore an ermine mantel.
She never wore shoes
Unless they were made of cordovan leather.
They were decorated with gold and silver
And cords of silk with which she fastened them.
She was so good looking
That she turned everyone's head.
The foolish and the wise
All thought she was of noble parentage.
She was so good a conversationalist
And she had so attractive a body
That the son of the emperor
Took her as his wife.
All the people of the city
Loved her for her beauty.
All said: 'It is such a shame
About this woman of noble lineage.
She seems learned about all things.
Why does she live such a life?
This young lady should weep
For she was so well born'.

[VII. MARY SEEKS PASSAGE ON A SHIP]

One day in the month of May
This Mary got up
And went to the city wall
To show off her beauty.
She looked down on the gates
Where she was accustomed to play her games.
She saw a galley arriving
Upon the sea;
It was full of pilgrims,
There were no poor people there.
It was full of pilgrims
Of rich men and knights.
All were going on a pilgrimage
To Jerusalem with a favorable wind.
They were in a hurry to go
Because they wanted to be there
For a feast which comes once a year,
Great and universal.
It was the day of the Ascension
When a great pilgrimage took place.
There in that place they paused,
Because they wanted to eat there;
There they sought a brief rest
Thinking that afterward they would go on.
There were there some frivolous young men,
Who went hand in hand.
They began to walk;
They went along the shore amusing themselves,
Running along the seashore,
Playing in the sand.
When Mary noticed them,
She could not keep from laughing.
Near her she saw a man standing;
She began to ask him:
'For God's sake tell me, Sir,

If you have love for God,
These men who came out of the great ship,
Where do they come from or who are they?
If I could go with them,
I would like very much to leave here.
I want to leave this place;
I have no desire to stay here'.
Then the man answered her—
The one she had asked—saying:
'This I know for certain,
That they are going to Jerusalem.
If you had something to give them
They could take you'.
She answered him:
'I have a good body', she said;
'I will give it freely,
But I will give them no other gift,
Because I have only one coin'.
The man heard this madness,
He could not keep from laughing.
When he heard what she said, the young man
Left her there and took his leave.
Mary got up.
No one was there to give her advice.
She was wearing alexandrian cloth.
She held in her hand a lark,
(In this country they call it a finch.
There they have no such singing bird).
In her hand she took it.
Quickly she descended the wall.
She was so beside herself
That she did not turn in at her lodging.
She began to run very fast,
As if she were carried by the wind.
She ran down the street.
Quickly she came to the shore.
She greeted the young men;

She laid bare to them her heart.
'God save you, lads,
You seem to me like good men.
I was born in a distant land,
And now I am a confused woman.
I was born in the land of Egypt,
And here I have been without support.
I have no friend or relative,
Things are going badly and sadly.
I tell you on oath
That I have neither gold nor silver.
I swear to you by the true God
That I have with me only one coin.
Here is my treasure,
All my silver and gold.
If you will agree to put me on the boat,
To serve you gladly
I will go with you to the Holy Land
If you choose to take me.
By taking along one woman
You will not leave shore any later.
If you can do this act of almsgiving,
You will arrive more quickly.
For God I ask you, for charity,
That you take me with you'.
When they heard her entreaty,
There was no one who said no.
They took her in their hands,
They placed her on the ship.

[VIII. VOYAGE TO PALESTINE]

They began to row the boat;
They set out upon the sea.
Then they hoisted the sails.
All night they traveled by the stars.
No one sleeps there

Because Mary makes herself available.
First she tempts them,
Then she embraces them.
And when she goes to bed with them,
She kisses them with great passion.
There was no one there so thoughtful,
Neither youth or old man,
There was no one there so chaste
That he did not sin with her.
No one could restrain himself,
So alluring was her manner.
When she saw the great waves
So huge and deep
And the rain and high winds
Which accompanied the storms,
She felt no fear,
Nor did she call upon her Creator.
Rather she began to encourage them;
She invited them to romp.
So totally had the devil captivated her
That she went around all night scantily dressed.
She uncovered her hair,
No man had seen prettier.
They wanted her so much
That they did her every bidding.
One can wonder greatly,
That one woman had such an impact.
There was no night
That the devil was not with her.
He sought to entrap her
So she would perish in the sea.
But he did her no harm
Because God brought her to port.

[IX. MARY GOES TO JERUSALEM]

When Mary arrived
She was sad and troubled.
She was weeping along the beach.
The girl knew not what to do.
She knew neither man nor woman.
That land was totally unfamiliar.
She did not know how
She could live in that land.
In the end she said:
I will go to Jerusalem town.
I will return to my trade
So that I can take good care of myself.
Thus, weeping and confused
She entered Jerusalem.
There she did not stop sinning.
If anything, she became worse.
Now hear of her wantonness
Before the day of the Ascension.
She was so bad,
It would have been better had she not been born.[4]
The young men of the town
Were so won over by her beauty,
That all had their way with her.
Then came the day of the Ascension.
There was a great procession
Of pilgrims from across the sea,
Who came to pray in God's temple.
Good men and pilgrims
Came to the temple to pray to God.
Mary didn't care.
She joined in the company,
She walked in the procession,

[4]This translates *mejor le fuera non fuese nada.* One might read *nata* instead
of *nada.* The meaning remains essentially the same.

But for no good purpose.
When the pilgrims saw her,
They did not know what was in her heart.
If they had known who Mary was,
They would not have kept her company.
At the doors they came to the steps
And they entered the temple.

[X. MARY CANNOT ENTER]

The crowd went inside
But Mary did not go in.
She joined the pushing throng
But there was no way she could enter.
It seemed to her
That she saw many people
Who resembled knights,
But seemed very fierce.
Each of them had a sword
And threatened her at the entrance.
When she asked to enter inside,
They made her turn back.
When she saw she could not gain entry,
She turned back.

[XI. MARY'S PRAYER AT THE ICON]

Then she was very upset,
And sat down at a corner.
There she began to ponder
And to cry from her heart.
She pulled her hair with both hands;
She beat her breast.
She saw that God was angry
And she dared not ask for advice.
She said: 'In an evil hour
I was a great sinner.

I have listened to very bad advice,
While God has been so angry with me.
I am so full of wickedness,
Of lust and of evil,
That I cannot enter the church
Nor do I dare call upon God.
What will you do now, wretch?
I am sorry I'm alive!'
From her body arose a great sigh.
She said: God, let me die!"
She turned her face where she sat:
She saw an image of holy Mary.
The image was well fashioned
And well proportioned.
When Mary saw her,
She got to her feet and stood before her.
She knelt before her;
With great shame she looked at her.
Most devoutly she entreated her
And said: 'O Lady, sweet mother,
Who in your womb carried your father;
Saint Gabriel brought you the message;
You responded with great wisdom.
How good was that day
When he said to you: "Hail Mary".
God placed His love in you;
You were full of His grace.
In you humanity was taken up
By the Son of the King of Majesty.
What he said, that you granted
And called yourself his handmaid.
For this you are the queen of heaven.
Today you are my healer.
For my wounds, which are mortal,
I desire no other remedies.
If you with your Son attend me
I will be cured of these afflictions.

Listen to me, Lady, to what I tell you.
I am parting ways with the devil
And his minions
That I may not serve him in my days.
In your Son I will put my trust,
I wish to turn to penitence,
I wish to turn to my Lord.
I will put myself in your care.
All my life I will serve Him.
Never will I leave Him.
I will leave this life
Which I have led for so long
And I will always be repentant.
I will do severe penance.
Virgin Queen, I believe this of you,
That if you ask your Son for me,
If you request this gift,
I know I will have pardon.
Virgin, through whom so many wonders happen,
Obtain for me this pardon.
Virgin, virgin even after giving birth,
Obtain for me the love of your Son.
I believe, by my faith,
That God was in your giving birth.
From you he took his humanity,
But you did not lose your virginity.
It was a great miracle: the Father
Made his daughter his mother.
And it was a wondrous event,
That from the thorn budded the rose;
And from the rose blossomed the fruit
By which the whole world was saved.
You and I share a name,
But you are very different from me.
You are Mary and I am Mary
But the two of us have not the same life.
You always loved chastity,

And I, lewdness and evil.
The devil was your enemy;
He was my master and friend.
You are a most humble lady,
I am poor and haughty
And lecherous in my body.
Our Lord loved you,
And since he loved you,
Lady, have pity on me.
Lady, you have such a treasure
More precious than silver and gold.
In you the King of Heaven took flesh
As Saint John showed with his finger
When he addressed him: "Angel of God
Who will save us all'.'
When the enemy
Who cast us from paradise heard of it—
That he would have to save the whole world—
He sought to deceive him
Just as he had made Adam sin
When he cast him from paradise
Because of the apple he put in his mouth.
He tried to do the same to your Son,
But he was very sorry he tried.
Three times he tried,
But he gained nothing by it.
And when he saw he was so strongly armed
He led him to death by treachery.
But the death was very fortunate
For his life was restored.
And if he had not died,
No one would have obtained paradise.
But by dying he was empowered
To overcome the devil.
The Victim conquered the killer.
And showed the deceiver to be a traitor.
He broke the enclosures of hell

And broke open all its gates,
Then he led out those whom he sought
Whom the devil held inside.
He led outside his friends
Whom the devil had held captive within.
He led them there with great boldness.
He lifted them to heaven with great power.
He placed his body in the tomb.
He arose with great strength.
He appeared to his disciples;
With them he stayed forty days.
He taught them the new law
He kissed them on the mouth.
He entrusted them to his sweet mother.[5]
He rose to heaven to his Father.
From heaven he sent them strength
So they would not fear death.
He sent them the Holy Spirit
Who taught them all languages.
In heaven he sits at the right of his Father.
You, his sweet mother, are with him.
When the final judgment will come,
Which will judge the whole of this world,
You will be much honored
As lady most venerable
Crowned virgin queen.
You were once pregnant with your Son,
So you are all the more blessed,
A lady who had been a nobody,
When he sought to be born of you,
He who had to save the world.
Such is the truth
Such charity commands me today'.
When she had made her prayer,

---

[5]One could also interpret this: 'he entrusted his mother to them'.

She had pardon from God.
To God in heaven she made her prayer
That he protect her from temptation.

[XII. MARY SUBMITS TO GOD'S CALL]

Then she raised both her hands
And joined her two palms.
She signed herself with her right hand
When she had finished her prayer.
Mary got up from there;
She put her trust in her new Lord.
Without hesitation she returned to the church.
She saw no barrier.
The prayers she heard with great fervor.
She adored the cross of her Lord.
When she had adored it
She was inspired by God,
And she knew her calling
From God, and all that she should do.
Now cleansed from sins
She turned to the image.
She believed in it.
From it she asked advice about penance;
In what way she would subsist
Or to what place she should go.
She heard a voice most surely
Which told her clearly:
'Go to the bank of the River Jordan
To the monastery of Saint John.
You will receive healing.
You will be cured of all your sins.
They will give you the Body of Christ,
And they will take you across the River Jordan.
Then you will enter a desert.
You will stay there a long time.
You will be in the desert.

As long as you live, you will do penance there'.
When she heard this holy voice,
She made the sign of the cross on her forehead.

[XIII. JOURNEY TO THE JORDAN]

Mary took the road from there
And met a pilgrim.
She met a pilgrim there
Who gave her three crusts for God's sake.
She received them willingly,
The three loaves that he gave.
They were her sustenance
As long as she lived in penance.
Mary came to the River Jordan.
She took up residence there
On the bank of the River Jordan
Near the church of Saint John.
She lay down under a shelter
And ate half of one of the three loaves.
She drank the holy water.
When she drank it, she was totally satisfied.
In the water she bathed her head,
She felt herself cleansed from her sins.
However, she had made a great journey,
And she was disturbed.
On the hard ground, she made her bed.
She had there neither mattress nor mat.
She slept little; she couldn't sleep
Because the hard bed kept her awake.
She arose very early
In order to go hear the hours at the church.

[XIV. MARY A SOLITARY PILGRIM IN THE DESERT]

Later she boarded some barges;
She crossed the waters of the River Jordan.

When she passed to the other side,
She entered a great desert.
Mary never stopped traveling
Nor did she forget the queen
In whom she had placed her trust
Before the image of her Lord
Who in his mercy never abandoned her
And from the devil protected her.
In her she put her faith.
Now she began her penitence.
Although she felt she was dying from hunger,
She didn't want to change her mind.
Only two and a half loaves has she in her possession,
She knows that God will arrange it
That she be sustained by those few
If God does not send her further aid.
As much as she was able,
She kept traveling on.
As long as the day lasted
She never stopped.
When she had finished the day's journey
She found shelter under a tree.
She ate a little of her bread
And then she slept until morning.
The place did not seem suitable to her,
She wanted to keep going on and on.
In the morning Mary arose;
She set out toward the east.
Many nights and days she traveled.
She found many rough ways.
Finally she came to a mountainous region
Which became very cold and savage.
But she never forgot night and day
To call upon Holy Mary.
Constantly she remembered what she had said
And what she had proposed to her,
When she had entrusted herself to her

Before the image of her Lord.
There Mary came to a halt.
There she stayed for many years.
Her shoes and all her clothes
Lasted for seven years.
She spent the next forty years
Going naked without clothes.
In strong winds and great cold
She went naked without clothing.

[XV. PORTRAIT OF MARY THE PENITENT]

Her appearance changed completely.
She had neither clothes nor vesture.
She lost weight and color.
She became white as a flower.
Her hair which had been red
Turned white and grimy.
Her ears which were white
Became very black like tar.
Her eyes became bleary,
They had lost their sparkle.
The skin of her mouth drooped
And was blackened all about.
Her face was black and beaten
By the cold wind and the frost.
Her skin and her jaw
Looked like a burnt log.
Her chest was black
As tar and pitch,
Her breasts had no nipples
And, I surmise, were dry.
Her arms were long and her fingers dark;
When she held them out they resembled skewers.
Her nails were uneven;
She cut them with her teeth.
Her stomach was very shriveled

Because she never ate any food.
Her feet were chapped;
In many places they were injured.
She made no effort to avoid
The thorns which were found there.
She seemed at ease,
Nothing was wanting to her there.
When a thorn wounded her,
One of her sins was expiated;
And she was very glad
To suffer such a hard thing.
It is no wonder that she turned darker,
A woman who led such a life.
Nor is it surprising if her color changed
When she went about naked for forty years.

[XVI. LIFE IN THE MOUNTAINS]

She had three small loaves
Which were her food.
The first year they were as hard
As if they had been rocks in a wall.
After that they were white
As if they had been prepared that day.
Each day she ate some of them
But just a little bit.
When this bread was used up
Mary turned to the wild plants.
She chewed them like just another animal
But she was not bothered by that.
She traveled the mountains,
Eating the wild plants.
On plants and grains
She lived for eighteen years.
Afterward she lived for twenty years when she would not
have eaten
Had an angel not provided for her.

It is not to lament her sin
Of the body that she goes about so afflicted.
Before she had come to this place
The devil tried to tempt her
And to remind her of all
That she used to love:
The big dinners and good beds
Where she used to commit her sins.
But she was so fortunate
That she had forgotten it all.
All her life long
She did not remember her sin.
In all the mountains she saw
Nothing which was weird;
No evil creature
As she walked safely through the fields.
She stayed in many places.
If things went badly, it mattered little to her.
She was thinking about God, of nothing else.
Such was her spiritual life.

[XVII. THE MONASTERY OF SAINT JOHN]

Mary can rest here a little,
While you are told of an abbey
Which was on top of a mountain
And had a good community.
Never have you seen people
Whom you would honor for God so carefully.
They had wide crowns[6]
They wore tunics of skins.
They did not care about fabric of wool.
They were not found on beds or cots.

---

[6]The word is *coronas*. Taking his cue from the french text *(tant erent en grant descepline)*, Alvar suggests the meaning *sacrificios*. I suspect the meaning may be 'tonsures'.

To be cleansed of their sins
They wore no shoes.
Night and day they served God.
Know for certain that they did not sleep.
All day they were at their tasks
Until it was time to eat.
And when they went to eat,
They did not want much to do so.
They lived in poverty.
They did so for the love of God.
They ate barley bread and no other;
For certain they added no salt.
And when they held a great feast
They had acorns and a little fruit.
They drank unhealthy water
Which did not come from a spring.
Among them there was no greed
Nor envy nor avarice.
They were all men of good will
Who did not seek to possess property,
Nor did they want to have silver and gold
Because God was their treasure.
So holy was their life
That no man alive can describe it to you.

[XVIII. THE MONKS' LENTEN PRACTICE]

When Lent came
On the first day they had their evening meal.
Their abbot said Mass for them
And then gave them all communion.
After that he ate supper with them
And washed the feet of all.
Afterward he asked them to pray;
Then he gave them a sermon.
After he finished his preaching,
He had them exchange a kiss.

The abbot kissed them all
Then he opened the door of the church.
He sent them to the mountains,
He commended them to the God of heaven.
The holy monks took their leave from there,
All except two who stayed behind.
They stayed for no other love
Than to serve the Creator.
They stayed to say the hours
And to serve the church.
For when the church is without the hours
God is much saddened;
But the two were always there
To render service to God.
All the others left
To go to the mountains.
All had their hearts on God.
These disciples lived on plants.
When two happened to see each other
Each hastened away.
And when they happened to meet,
No one spoke to another.
Wherever night overtook them
There they all slept.
When they got up in the morning,
They signed themselves with the cross.
They commended themselves to the name of God,
Not knowing where they were traveling.
These same resolves
Were shared by all the disciples.
From all their eyes streamed tears unending
When they remembered the great judgment,
Where the angels will tremble
From the great fear that will shake them.
When the great and powerful king
They will see come in his majesty,
And in front of him, the burning fire

Where the devil keeps many people.
And many others will enter there
Who will never get out.
For this reason were the holy monks
Given to tears and loud laments.
To escape this danger
They uttered great sighs.
When they completed their Lent,
Before Maundy Thursday
On the Sunday of the Palms,
They returned to the monastery.
The holy abbot was very pleased
When he saw all of them there.
The shepherd is happy with his sheep
When they all come back unharmed.
He has them enter the monastery,
Then he has the doors shut.
The abbot, don John, cared for them well,
While another year passed.
And when the next year came,
The abbot did what was customary.
All went to the church;
He opened the doors; he sent them out.
He sent them to the mountains,
To the God of heaven he commended them.
The holy monks left there
And went to the mountains.
They did their penances there
But they were not together.

[XIX. THE MEETING OF ZOSIMAS AND MARY]

One of them turned to his right,
A man of very good life.
Don Zosimas was his name.
He was dressed in the garb of a monk.
You would not give for his clothing

One ripe apple,
But he considered it so precious
That he would not trade it for a horse.
His poverty was more precious to him
Than riches to a count.
He traveled far into the mountains
In order to find a hermit.
He wanted to find a hermit
With whom he could speak about God.
When he had traveled for ten days
Which was very tiring
He saw he was not able to find anyone,
And he did not want to go further.
It was the midday hour:
He said his hours; he adored God.
When he had finished his prayer
He turned to the right.
He turned his eyes to the east
And saw for sure a shadow;
He saw a shadow which was
Of a man or woman.
The vision was not illusory.
The shadow was of the Egyptian.
God had sent her
Whom He did not wish to be hidden.
God wished to disclose his treasure
Which was more precious than gold.
The holy man was puzzled;
He went quickly toward the shadow.
He wondered if it might be an apparition
Or some fantasy.
With his hand he blessed himself
And commended himself to God
That he might defend him from the demon
And from wicked temptation.
When his prayer was over,
He saw the figure of Mary.

It was clearly Mary's body
Without any clothing.
She was covered by no other garment
Than her hair, which was grown out.
Her hair, white as snow,
Covered her down to her feet.
She had no other clothing.
When the wind lifted her hair
Below there appeared her flesh burned
By the sun and the frost.
When the holy man saw her form,
He hurried toward her.
When Mary saw him coming
Immediately she began to flee.
The holy man followed after her.
He caught up with her a little.
He began to follow more intently
Because of his desire to speak with her.
For his heart told him
That this woman served God.

[XX. MUTUAL BLESSINGS]

He followed her across the mountain.
Quickly he reached her, saying:
'Lady, I want you to speak to me
For God is with you,
By God almighty I entreat you
Not to go away from here'.
When she heard him speak of God,
She immediately began to sign herself:
'Ah, my spiritual Lord,
For forty-seven years, by my reckoning,
I have not heard tell of You.
Now you have sent a holy man
And I dare not turn my face.
I dare not turn my body toward him

Because I am completely naked'.
She stayed there in that place,
But she did not dare to turn her face.
She began to speak with him
Because she did not want to hide any more.
'Sir', she said, 'friend of God,
I would be glad to speak with you,
Because I know you would give me good advice
And that your name is Zosimas.
But I am a naked creature
Who has no clothes at all.
If you will give me one of your garments
I will tell you what you want to know'.
When Zosimas heard her say his name
He knew that God had enabled her to say it
Since she did not know his name
And there was no one there to tell her.
He saw that the Holy Spirit had revealed to her
What she had spoken.
The holy man readily agreed
And gave her one of his garments.
He turned away
Until the lady was clothed.
After she was dressed
She approached the holy man.
'Sir', she said, 'friend of God,
Where have you come from?
In God's name I ask you to tell me
Where did you come from and what do you seek?
Here am I, a penitent
Who travels through the desert grieving
For the great sins I did
Which are so filthy and oppressive.
I am doing heavy penance for them,
I am here in repentance'.
When the holy man heard what she said,
Moved by compassion he began to cry.

He cast himself at the feet of the lady,
He asked for her blessing.
The lady acted politely,
She threw herself at the feet of the holy man.
She began to weep copiously
And at once to speak.
And he did something similar.
There you will see much weeping.
Don Zosimas lies on the ground,
The tears run down his face
With great anguish, totally drenched is
His beard which is gray.
May she pray for the people
And then give him her blessing.
Mary raised her eyes a little,
She said to the holy man:
'Friend, lord and companion:
I should have it first;
You ask for blessing
But I think that is not right.
You are a cleric who celebrates Mass
And you put your hands on the altar,
And by your sign of blessing
God manifests great miracles.
The bread becomes his flesh
And wine turns into his blood.
God takes account of your sacrifice;
All your life he has taken.
There is no lechery in you,
No greed, no avarice.
It will be quite certain
That by your hand I will be blessed.
You can trust in your Lord
Because you always served him with honor.
Since you have from him great reward,
Now you may give me your blessing'.
Then Zosimas answered her:

'I see great signs:
I will not get up from here
If I do not have your blessing.
Not for hunger or thirst
Will I arise from here,
Nor for any other reason
Until you give me your blessing'.
When Mary saw what was in the heart
Of the good man Zosimas,
That he would keep entreating
Until she gave her blessing,
She then began a prayer,
Her eyes filled with heartfelt tears.
Devoutly, with great love,
She asked the Lord:
'God', she said, 'sweet Creator,
You are the Lord of heaven and earth.
I praise you and I adore you.
And in you I have all my treasure.
Send your blessing
Upon me and upon this man.
Give us pardon for our sins
And give us your blessing'.
Don Zosimas rose to his feet:
'Ah, Lord, who are in heaven,
If it pleases you and you wish it
Give us your pardon.
Free us from these punishments.
Place us in heaven where you reign'.
Mary said: 'Amen'.

[XXI. NEWS OF THE WORLD]

Then she asked what was on her mind.
She asked him about many things,
And the holy man taught her about them.
She asked him about the kings,

If they kept their laws,
And how they kept their lands,
Whether at peace or in war.
The pastors who defend the law,
How they were and how they kept it.
Then don Zosimas answered:
'Throughout the land there is great peace.
There is no one in our land
Who would dare to start a war.
But as for mother church it is fitting
That you pray for her'.
'May God give her virtue
And preserve her in peace and salvation'.

[XXII. MARY'S LEVITATION]

She turned her eyes toward the east.
She lifted her hands and raised them to heaven.
The lips of her mouth moved,
But no word came out.
She was lifted from the earth
One full step
So that between her and the ground
There were two and a half feet.
When don Zosimas saw her
He fell back with great fear
And prayed to God
That he receive her gladly.
But Zosimas was very afraid
And called upon his Creator.
He thought she was a phantom
So he moved a little away from where he was.

[XXIII. MARY'S CONFESSION]

When she saw him drawing back,
She began to call:

'Don Zosimas, why did you draw back?
Friend, tell me, why are you in doubt?
Do not be perplexed by what God is doing here.
I am a Christian, as it pleases him.
I was baptized in childhood.
I believe in God and holy Mary.
In God I put my faith
So that here I am in penitence.
I do not want to leave here
Until the hour of my death'.
Saying this, she lifted her hand
And devoutly blessed herself.
The holy man saw this
And fell at her feet.
The holy woman reached out to raise him up
Before she began to cry.
'Lady', said don Zosimas,
'Tell me: Where are you from and why are you here?
From what land do you come?
For God's sake, tell me about your life.
Tell it to me in confession,
So God may give you true pardon'.
Mary said: 'Yes, I will tell you,
Be assured that I won't hide anything.
I will give you my account in such a way
That nothing will be hidden.
Since you have seen my naked flesh,
I will hide nothing of my life from you'.
At this point she began to tell her story.
She did not want to hide anything.
She told him her whole life
From the day she was born.
But when she had told it,
He knew she was seized with great shame.
She told all of it there;
She lay at his feet, she asked for pardon.
When she had said what she had done,

She fell on the ground at his feet.
When the holy man saw her,
He pleaded with the Creator.
He gave thanks to the Creator.
He asked the lady with great affection:
'Lady, why do you fall at my feet?
For God's sake I beg you to arise
Though I do not know by what right of rank
Nor by what authority.
In what I heard you tell
And in what I see arising in your eyes,
Never have I seen your equal;
For God's sake, advise me here.
Lady, I ask you for advice,
Whether I could stay with you'.

[XXIV. MARY'S ADVICE, PROPHECY, AND REQUEST]

'No, my Lord, don Zosimas',
The lady said to him, 'You will go away instead,
And you will not return here again.
It is not necessary to tell my life to you
Right up to my death.
When God showed me to you,
I sought to be counseled by you.
You will go to the abbot, don John,
You will deliver this message:
Let him take care of his sheep,
That he may know they are very safe:
Let him take counsel about caring for them
Because there is much to amend.
But when that time comes,
You will be sick, know it for certain.
All your companions
Will go from their cells;
All your companions will leave
And go to the mountains.

You will not be able to go with them
So you will have to stay behind.
They will return when the time comes
According to their custom,
When Lent has passed
And the day of the [Last] Supper has come.
You will be healed, I think.
I ask you for one more thing:
Into a clear vessel
Place the Body of Jesus Christ,
And some of the Blood in another vessel
Which has been well cleaned.
You will carry it with you
And you will find me close by
For I will go to it eagerly
And when I see it I will be glad.
At the River Jordan on the bank
There you will find me, otherwise wait for me there.
I wish to receive communion;
I will come near for it
From where the River Jordan passes
Behind the church of Saint John.
I have not received the Body of my Lord
And because of that I am very sad.
I have seen no one besides you.
I wish to go. Pray for me'.

[XXV. ZOSIMAS DEPARTS; HIS RETURN A YEAR LATER]

After she said this she left him
And set out for the mountains.
When the holy man saw her leave,
He knew that he could not stay;
Through the desert, on pathways,
He immediately returned to his companions.
When the holy abbot saw them
He did what was customary.

The holy abbot watched over them there
Until a year had passed.
Don Zosimas knew it was true
What Mary had said to him.
Then he passed Lent
Until the day of the Supper came round.
Then Zosimas felt well,
He took the Body of the Lord in his hand.
Dom Zosimas prepared to go, taking
A little barley and lentils with him.
To the bank of the River Jordan
He followed the road:
He thought to find Mary
But she had not yet arrived there to meet him.
'God', he said, 'in whom I believe,
Let me see what I desire'.

[XXVI. SECOND MEETING. COMMUNION]

He saw her there on the other side.
Then he began to speak:
'Lady', said Zosimas,
'My dear mother, what will you do?'
When Mary heard him say this,
She had no hesitations.
Mary came across the water
As if she were coming on a road.
She arrived dry on the bank.
Don Zosimas saluted her then.
She cast herself down at his feet
And asked him for a blessing.
He did not dare to bless her,
But helped her arise.
He raised her from the earth
And greeted her with the holy peace.
'Lady, I tell you plainly,
You know that this is not bread.

This is the Body of Jesus Christ
Who for us accepted martyrdom
And both death and suffering
And gave us great salvation.
Do you believe this, my friend?'
'I believe it well', said Mary.
'For the great sin that Adam committed,
For the apple he placed in his mouth.
This blood He has given us,
Mad is whoever holds it of no account'.
He gave it to her; she received it.
She ate the flesh, drank the blood.
When Mary had received communion,
She was joyful and well satisfied.

[XXVII. NUNC DIMITTIS]

She turned her face toward the east
And asked almighty God:
'Lord God, hear my prayer;
I wish to ask you a favor:
For forty-seven years I have served you.
May you have pity on me.
Now I would ask for the reward
That you have prepared for me.
Ask your Son, O Virgin Mary,
To set me in your company
And I will sing the sweet song
That Solomon sang of you.
For the pleasure of this life
All turns to great sadness'.
When she had finished her prayer,
She turned to the holy man:
'Lord Zosimas', she said:
'Sweet friend, what will you do?
By the grace of God and Holy Mary
You have completed your pilgrimage.

In that exact place
Where you first found me,
There you will find me'.
'Yes, I will do it', said Zosimas,
'But if you wish to give me great pleasure,
You will eat of this fruit'.
He gave it to her with both hands.
Mary took the three grains.
She drank of the water, but not because of thirst.
'Sir', she said to him, 'turn away from here.
I wish to leave you now.
For God's sake, I beg you, pray for me'.

[XXVIII. MARY'S DEATH]

In a moment she had crossed the river.
Quickly she traveled
To that exact place
Where Zosimas had first found her.
To that place which is worth more
Than balsam, which is a natural ointment.
When Mary was settled in that place,
She concluded a prayer.
She turned to the east;
She commended herself to almighty God.
She began to pray
Devoutly from her heart.
'God', she said, 'if you will hear me
I would like not to go from here'.
When she finished her prayer,
She saw a beautiful vision:
'I see good emissaries there.
I commend my body and soul to you'.
When she lay down on the ground,
Then He was with her.
Lying on the ground,
She commended herself to God,

Wrapped in her hair.
She put her arms on her breast;
She closed her tired eyes.
She shut her mouth and covered her teeth.
Her soul left her.
The angels received her.
The angels carry her as they go,
As they go singing a sweet song.
But you could swear to this:
The devil could not reach her.
This lady gives an example
For all who are in this world.

[XXIX. MARY'S BURIAL]

Don Zosimas took to the road,
He returned to his monastery.
But in one matter he was very disappointed:
Why had he not asked her for her name?
This weighed heavy on Zosimas
While Lent was slow in coming.
But when that season arrived,
The abbot gave them his blessing.
After Zosimas left,
He went quickly to the River Jordan.
He passed to the bank on the other side.
He took the road to Mary.
'O God', he said, 'show me her corpse.
I know for certain that she is dead'.
God wished well for Zosimas.
He did not want him to suffer any more.
He turned his eyes to the right.
And saw a brightness;
Toward that light he moved.
He saw the body; he was very glad.
It lay toward the east
With its eyes tightly closed.

Her hair served as her shroud.
Zosimas felt great compassion.
He took off one of his garments;
Reaching her body, he used it to cover her.
He looked down toward her head.
He saw some letters written on the ground.
They were very clear and well formed
Because they were formed in heaven.
Don Zosimas read them quickly,
As if they were on parchment.
'Zosimas, take the body of Mary;
Bury it this very day.
When you have buried it,
Pray for her, because she commended herself to you'.
When Zosimas discovered her name,
He was very grateful to God.
Afterward he held a service for her
And said the psalms from the psalter.
For one other reason was he sad.
Because he had brought nothing with him
With which he could open the ground
In order to bury the body.
For love of this Mary,
God sent him great help.
A lion came out of the mountains
To keep Zosimas company.
Although he was a wild animal,
Meekly he came where the body was.
He indicated he would help with the body,
Because he wished to aid in its burial.
When the good man saw this,
It cheered his heart.
Then he said to him: 'You, sweet friend,
Will stay here with me'.
The lion dug in the hard earth.
The holy man showed him the dimensions.
The grave was quickly dug out

And emptied of earth.
Both of them place her in the grave
And get out of it.
Don Zosimas gives the commendation
Without help from the lion.
But when he saw him throw the earth
He did not want to be there idle.
He carried all the dirt
And threw it on the body.
He cast himself on the ground in order to say good bye.
He made signs that he wished to go.
'Companion, go in peace.
I know well what God is doing for Mary'.
Then the lion left him
And went into the mountains.
'Now I believe by my faith
What a holy thing is penitence,
To do penance
And not to have pity on my body'.

[XXX. ZOSIMAS TELLS MARY'S STORY TO THE MONKS]

They returned to their abbey,
Zosimas and his community.
There they were speaking with good reason;
No evil intent was there.
Don Zosimas began to speak;
He did not wish to be quiet any longer.
He had not forgotten the Egyptian;
Her whole story he told them.
How he found her
When he went to the mountains,
And how he found her
After the end of the third year.
He told them about the lion,
How he had it as his companion.
The holy abbot wept copiously,

When he heard him tell of her death.
And the monks who were there
All cried also.

[XXXI. FINAL EXHORTATION]

They amended their lives greatly
Because of the example of this Mary.
And let us mend our lives also,
We have much need of it.
And let us ask this Mary
Every night and every day
That she entreat the Creator
With whom she shared deep love.
Let us do this service
So that on the day of judgment
We will not be found to be in wickedness.
May he give us a great share
In everlasting life.
Let every thinking person
Answer and say, 'Amen'.

CISTERCIAN PUBLICATIONS

Texts and Studies in the Monastic Tradition

TEXTS IN ENGLISH TRANSLATION

THE CISTERCIAN MONASTIC TRADITION

Aelred of Rievaulx

- Dialogue on the Soul
- The Historical Works
- Liturgical Sermons, I
- The Lives of the Northern Saints
- Spiritual Friendship
- Treatises I: Jesus at the Age of Twelve; Rule for a Recluse; Pastoral Prayer
- Walter Daniel: The Life of Aelred of Rievaulx

Bernard of Clairvaux

- Apologia to Abbot William (Cistercians and Cluniacs)
- Five Books on Consideration: Advice to a Pope
- Homilies in Praise of the Blessed Virgin Mary
- In Praise of the New Knighthood
- Letters
- Life and Death of Saint Malachy the Irishman
- On Baptism and the Office of Bishops
- On Grace and Free Choice
- On Loving God
- Parables and Sentences
- Sermons for the Summer Season
- Sermons on Conversion
- Sermons on the Song of Songs, I-IV
- The Steps of Humility and Pride

Gertude the Great of Helfta

- Spiritual Exercises
- The Herald of God's Loving-Kindness, Books 1 and 2
- The Herald of God's Loving-Kindness, Book 3

William of Saint Thierry

- The Enigma of Faith
- Exposition on the Epistle to the Romans
- Exposition on the Song of Songs
- The Golden Epistle
- The Mirror of Faith
- The Nature and Dignity of Love
- On Contemplating God, Prayer, Meditations

Gilbert of Hoyland

- Sermons on the Song of Songs, I-III
- Treatises, Sermons, and Epistles

John of Ford

- Sermons on the Final Verses of the Song of Songs, I-VII

Other Cistercian Writers

- Adam of Perseigne, Letters, I
- Alan of Lille: The Art of Preaching
- Amadeus of Lausanne: Homilies in Praise of Blessed Mary
- Baldwin of Ford: Commendation of Faith
- Geoffrey of Auxerre: On the Apocalypse
- Guerric of Igny: Liturgical Sermones, I-II
- Helinand of Froidmont: Verses on Death
- Idung of Prüfening: Cistercians and Cluniacs. The Case of Cîteaux
- In The School of Love. An Anthology of Early Cistercian Texts
- Isaac of Stella: Sermons on the Christian Year, I-[II]
- The Letters of Armand-Jean de Rancé, Abbot of la Trappe
- The Life of Beatrice of Nazareth
- Mary Most Holy: Meditating with the Early Cistercians
- Ogier of Locedio: Homilies [on Mary and the Last Supper]
- Serlo of Wilton & Serlo of Savigny: Seven Unpublished Works (Latin-English)
- Sky-blue the Sapphire, Crimson the Rose: The Spirituality of John of Ford
- Stephen of Lexington: Letters from Ireland
- Stephen of Sawley: Treatises
- Three Treatises on Man: A Cistercian Anthropology / Bernard McGinn

EARLY AND EASTERN MONASTICISM

- Besa: The Life of Shenoute of Atripe
- Cyril of Scythopolis: The Lives of the Monks of Palestine
- Dorotheos of Gaza: Discourses and Sayings
- Evagrius Ponticus: Praktikos and Chapters on Prayer
- Handmaids of the Lord: Lives of Holy Women in Late Antiquity and the Early Middle Ages / Joan Petersen
- Harlots of the Desert. A Study of Repentance / Benedicta Ward
- Isaiah of Scete: Ascetic Discourses

- John Moschos: The Spiritual Meadow
- The Life of Antony (translated from Coptic and Greek)
- The Lives of the Desert Fathers. The *Historia monachorum in Aegypto*
- The Spiritually Beneficial Tales of Paul, Bishop of Monembasia
- Symeon the New Theologian: The Practical and Theological Chapters, and The Three Theological Discourses
- Theodoret of Cyrrhus: A History of the Monks of Syria
- Stewards of the Poor. [Three biographies from fifth-century Edessa]
- The Syriac Book of Steps *[Liber graduum]*
- The Syriac Fathers on Prayer and the Spiritual Life / Sebastian Brock

LATIN MONASTICISM

- Achard of Saint Victor: Works
- Anselm of Canterbury: Letters, I–III
- Bede the Venerable: Commentary on the Acts of the Apostles
- Bede the Venerable: Commentary on the Seven Catholic Epistles
- Bede the Venerable: Homilies on the Gospels, I–II
- Bede the Venerable: Excerpts from the Works of Saint Augustine on the Letters of the Blessed Apostle Paul
- The Celtic Monk [An Anthology]
- Gregory the Great: Forty Gospel Homilies
- Guigo II: The Ladder of Monks and Twelve Meditations / Colledge, Walsh edd.
- Halfway to Heaven
- The Life of the Jura Fathers
- The Maxims of Stephen of Muret
- Peter of Celle: Selected Works
- The Letters of Armand-Jean de Rancé, I–II
- The Rule of the Master
- The Rule of Saint Augustine
- Saint Mary of Egypt. Three Medieval Lives in Verse

STUDIES IN MONASTICISM / CISTERCIAN STUDIES

Cistercian Studies and Reflections

- Aelred of Rievaulx. A Study / Aelred Squire
- Athirst for God. Spiritual Desire in Bernard of Clairvaux's Sermons on the Song of Songs / Michael Casey
- Beatrice of Nazareth in her Context, I–II: Towards Unification with God / Roger DeGanck
- Bernard of Clairvaux. Man. Monk. Mystic / Michael Casey
- The Cistercian Way / André Louf
- Dom Gabriel Sortais. An Amazing Abbot in Turbulent Times / Guy Oury
- The Finances of the Cistercian Order in the Fourteenth Century / Peter King
- Fountains Abbey and Its Benefactors / Joan Wardrop
- A Gathering of Friends. Learning and Spirituality in John of Ford
- Hidden Springs: Cistercian Monastic Women, 2 volumes
- Image of Likeness. The Augustinian Spirituality of William of St Thierry / D. N. Bell
- Index of Authors and Works in Cistercian Libraries in Great Britain / D. N. Bell

- Index of Cistercian Authors and Works in Medieval Library catalogues in Great Britain / D. N. Bell
- The Mystical Theology of Saint Bernard / Etienne Gilson
- The New Monastery. Texts and Studies on the Earliest Cistercians
- Monastic Odyssey [Cistercian Nuns & the French Revolution]
- Nicolas Cotheret's Annals of Cîteaux / Louis J. Lekai
- Pater Bernhardus. Martin Luther and Bernard of Clairvaux / Franz Posset
- Rancé and the Trappist Legacy / A. J. Krailsheimer
- A Second Look at Saint Bernard / Jean Leclercq
- The Spiritual Teachings of St Bernard of Clairvaux / John R. Sommerfeldt
- Studies in Medieval Cistercian History
- Three Founders of Cîteaux / Jean-Baptiste Van Damme
- Understanding Rancé. Spirituality of the Abbot of La Trappe in Context / D. N. Bell
- William, Abbot of Saint Thierry
- Women and Saint Bernard of Clairvaux / Jean Leclercq

Cistercian Art, Architecture, and Music

- Cistercian Abbeys of Britain [illustrated]
- Cistercian Europe / Terryl N. Kinder
- Cistercians in Medieval Art / James France
- SS. Vincenzo e Anastasio at Tre Fontane Near Rome / J. Barclay Lloyd
- Studies in Medieval Art and Architecture, II–VI / Meredith P. Lillich, ed.
- Treasures Old and New. Nine Centuries on Cistercian Music [CD, cassette]
- Cistercian Chants for the Feast of the Visitation [CD]

Monastic Heritage

- Community and Abbot in the Rule of St Benedict, I–II / Adalbert de Vogüé
- Distant Echoes: Medieval Religious Women, I / Shank, Nichols, edd.
- The Freedom of Obedience / A Carthusian
- Halfway to Heaven [The Carthusian Tradition] / Robin Lockhart
- The Hermit Monks of Grandmont / Carole A. Hutchison
- A Life Pleasing to God: Saint Basil's Monastic Rules / Augustine Holmes
- Manjava Skete [Ruthenian tradition] / Sophia Seynk
- Monastic Practices / Charles Cummings
- Peace Weavers. Medieval Religious Women, II / Shank, Nichols, edd.
- Reading Saint Benedict / Adalbert de Vogüé
- The Rule of St Benedict. A Doctrinal and Spiritual Commentary / Adalbert de Vogüé
- Stones Laid Before the Lord [Monastic Architecture] / Anselme Dimier
- What Nuns Read [Libraries of Medieval English Nunneries] / D. N. Bell

Monastic Liturgy

- From Advent to Pentecost / A Carthusian
- The Hymn Collection from the Abbey of the Paraclete, 2 volumes
- The Molesme Summer Season Breviary, 4 volumes
- The Old French Ordinary and Breviary of the Abbey of the Paraclete, 5 volumes
- The Paraclete Statutes: *Institutiones nostrae*
- The Twelfth Century Cistercian Hymnal, 2 volumes
- The Twelfth Century Cistercian Psalter [NYP]
- Two Early Cistercian *Libelli Missarum*

MODERN MONASTICISM

Thomas Merton

- Cassian and the Fathers: Initiation into the Monastic Tradition
- The Climate of Monastic Prayer
- The Legacy of Thomas Merton
- The Message of Thomas Merton
- The Monastic Journey of Thomas Merton
- Thomas Merton Monk
- Thomas Merton on Saint Bernard
- Thomas Merton: Prophet of Renewal / John Eudes Bamberger
- Toward An Integrated Humanity [Essays on Thomas Merton]

Contemporary Monastics

- Centered on Christ. A Guide to Monastic Profession / Augustine Roberts
- Inside the Psalms. Reflections for Novices / Maureen McCabe
- Passing from Self to God. A Cistercian Retreat / Robert Thomas
- Pathway of Peace. Cistercian Wisdom according to Saint Bernard / Charles Dumont
- Poor Therefore Rich / A Carthusian
- The Way of Silent Love / A Carthusian

CHRISTIAN SPIRITUALITY PAST AND PRESENT

Past

- A Cloud of Witnesses. The Development of Christian Doctrine [to 500] / D. N. Bell
- Eros and Allegory: Medieval Exegesis of the Song of Songs / Denys Turner
- High King of Heaven. Aspects of Early English Spirituality / Benedicta Ward
- In the Unity of the Holy Spirit. Conference on the Rule of Benedict
- The Life of St Mary Magdalene and of Her Sister St Martha [Magdalene legend]
- The Luminous Eye. The Spiritual World Vision of St Ephrem / Sebastian Brock
- Many Mansions. Medieval Theological Development East and West / D. N. Bell
- The Name of Jesus / Irénée Hausherr
- Penthos. The Doctrine of Compunction in the Christian East / Irénée Hausherr

CISTERCIAN PUBLICATIONS Titles Listing

EDITORIAL OFFICES

Cistercian Publications • WMU Station
1903 West Michigan Avenue
Kalamazoo, MI 49008-5415   USA
tel 269 387 8920   fax 269 387 8390
e-mail cistpub@wmich.edu

CUSTOMER SERVICE—NORTH AMERICA: USA AND CANADA

Cistercian Publications at Liturgical Press
Saint John's Abbey
Collegeville, MN 56321-7500 USA
tel 800 436 8431   fax 320 363 3299
e-mail sales@litpress.org

CUSTOMER SERVICE—EUROPE: UK, IRELAND, AND EUROPE

Cistercian Publications at Columba Book Service
55A Spruce Avenue
Stillorgan Industrial Park
Blackrock, Co. Dublin, Ireland
tel 353 1 294 2560   fax 353 1 294 2564
e-mail sales@columba.ie

WEBSITE
www.cistercianpublications.org

Cistercian Publications is a non-profit corporation.